30-MIN...

SOCIAL MEDIA

MARKETING

Step-by-Step Techniques
to Spread the Word
About Your Business
FAST AND FREE

Susan Gunelius

**Mc
Graw
Hill**

New York Chicago San Francisco Lisbon London Madrid Mexico City
Milan New Delhi San Juan Seoul Singapore Sydney Toronto

To Scott, for supporting every new opportunity I pursue on and off the social Web and for sending me blog post ideas when I'm too busy to think straight. And to my family and friends for remembering me and welcoming me with open arms when I eventually emerge from behind my computer.

   3 4 5 6 7 8 9 10 11 12 13 14 15   QFR/QFR   1 9 8 7 6 5 4 3 2 1

ISBN   978-0-07-174381-5
MHID   0-07-174381-2

Library of Congress Cataloging-in-Publication Data

Gunelius, Susan.
      30-minute social media marketing : step-by-step techniques to spread the word about
   your business fast and free/ by Susan Gunelius.
         p.   cm.
      Includes bibliographical references.
      ISBN 978-0-07-174381-5 (alk.paper)
      1. Internet marketing.   2. Online social networks.   I. Title.   II. Title: Thirty-
   minute social media marketing.

      HF5415.1265.G86   2011
      658.8′72—dc22   2010026266

Interior design by Susan H. Hartman

Facebook® is a registered trademark of Facebook, Inc.

McGraw-Hill books are available at special quantity discounts to use as premiums and sales promotions or for use In corporate training programs. To contact a representative, please e-mail us at bulksales@mcgraw-hill.com.

This book is printed on acid-free paper.

Contents

PART I

Get Started: The Who, What, and Why of Social Media Marketing

PART II

Test the Water: The Where of Social Media Marketing

Foreword

Right now, your competitors are using social media tools to advance their personal and corporate brands, generate revenue, increase customer loyalty, and recruit top talent in order to gain leverage in your industry. Do you want to be shut out and close your operations? A few years ago, social media tools could give you a clear advantage in the marketplace, but now they are mandatory for reaching customers, building relationships, and becoming a recognized name. In 2008, cause-related marketing firm Cone (www.coneinc.com) released a study stating that 93 percent of Americans believe companies should have a social media presence, and 85 percent believe companies should also interact and engage with their audience.

It is 2010 now! These numbers must be nearing 100 percent, which means that just having profiles on Twitter and Facebook isn't enough. You actually have to know how to use them and understand the best practices and the best ways to implement them in your company. Technology is changing rapidly, and if you aren't keeping up-to-date with the latest trends, it's going to really hurt your business. No one had even heard of Twitter in 2006, but today it has about 106 million users, and it receives more media attention than Kim Kardashian, Britney Spears, and Brad Pitt combined. Most marketers have embraced Twitter at the expense of other tools that might be just as, if not more, powerful and rewarding. Just because there are a lot of online tools now, that doesn't mean traditional marketing tactics have lost their value. For instance, marketers are investing more than they ever have in direct marketing through targeted e-mail campaigns.

Social media is revolutionary and has changed our culture because it has leveled the media playing field and demolished corporate hierarchies. Now you can interact with executives without going through public relations, and sell products directly to your audience without begging the *New York Times* to write about you. It cuts through geography, race, gender, and age. It actually allows you to measure your own success immediately, in contrast to other media, which only let you estimate conversion. As incredible as social media is, it requires substantial time, patience, creativity, and commitment. I believe *commitment* is the key word for successfully using social media to market your brand because it takes into account the passion, energy, hard work, and long-term plan you'll need to achieve business results.

It's easy to tell a company to make time for updating social networks with fresh content and insights every single day, yet most find the effort overwhelming at the beginning. This is especially true since companies are bombarded with so many different social technologies, including blogging, microblogging, social networking, social bookmarking, video and audio podcasting, e-books, and more. Susan Gunelius has taken this common frustration and developed an easy, thoughtful, and strategic manual for your social media marketing success plan.

Avoid reading this social media marketing guide at your own peril!

—Dan Schawbel

#1 international bestselling author of *Me 2.0*, *BusinessWeek* columnist, and managing partner of Millennial Branding, LLC

Preface

Congratulations! By reading this book, you've taken the first step toward joining the social Web community and building your business in ways people only could have dreamed about a decade ago. No longer is your business limited to communicating with small audiences and growing locally. Today you can speak with people around the world and grow your business exponentially, all from the comfort of your own home, office, or store. As long as you have access to the Internet, you can use the tools of the social Web to build relationships and grow your business. In fact, there has never been a more exciting time to market a business than the 21st century.

This book introduces you not only to the tools of social media marketing but also to the fundamental marketing theories you need to understand in order to develop an effective social media marketing strategy and meet your goals. Social media marketing requires a shift in thinking in terms of how you communicate with consumers, but those basic marketing theories still apply. In other words, anyone can learn how to use the tools of social media marketing, but without a background or knowledge of basic marketing, you're just going through the motions without knowing why and without a fully defined strategy. Sure, you can get lucky and find social media success, but wouldn't you rather base your efforts on the fundamentals of marketing and consumer behavior theory than on luck?

This book takes the concept of social media marketing a step further than simply teaching you how to create a Twitter account or set up a blog. When you're done reading this book, you'll understand why you should even consider creating a Twitter account and how your business can benefit from having a blog. Don't market blindly. Read and understand the concepts in this book before you dive into social media marketing. The last thing you want to do is waste time or make a mistake, which can do more harm to your business than good.

Most important, remember that every business is different, and that means every business measures social media marketing success against its own objectives and standards. If your competitor has 10,000 Twitter followers, that's not a reason that you need to get 11,000 Twitter followers. In other words, don't market scared on the social Web. Instead, analyze what your competitors are doing on the social Web, analyze your target audience's needs, and analyze your own goals. Having 11,000 Twitter followers might not help you meet your goals at all.

This book is filled with step-by-step instructions, sample marketing plans, real-world examples, and quick-start success plans, so you'll be able to confidently join the online conversation before you even read the last page. Armed with the knowledge of marketing theory, along with the steps to use social media tools, you'll be able to create, test, and tweak your own social media marketing strategy and plan without feeling overwhelmed or intimidated.

Don't forget, no one knows everything about social media marketing, and no one has identified the recipe for social media marketing success. Given that social media marketing is free or relatively inexpensive, the risk to leveraging the online conversation to build your business is negligible. In fact, the bigger risk to your business is *not* joining the online conversation.

So what are you waiting for? Do you want to grow your business? Then start reading and learn how to reach your business goals through social media marketing!

Connect with Susan Gunelius on the Social Web

Blogs: www.keysplashcreative.com *and* www.womenonbusiness .com

Twitter: www.twitter.com/susangunelius *and* www.twitter.com/ womenonbusiness

Facebook: www.facebook.com/susangunelius *and* www.facebook .com/keysplashcreative

LinkedIn: www.linkedin.com/in/susangunelius

Acknowledgments

Every book I write could never make it into readers' hands if it weren't for a long list of people who make it a reality. The first people who need to be acknowledged for helping to bring this book to publication are my agent, Bob Diforio, who thought of me when he heard about this book concept, and Michelle Wells at McGraw-Hill, who believed I could write it when Bob introduced me to her. I'm a firm believer in the power of the social Web to build a business (I'm a living example of the fact that social media marketing works), and this book gave me the opportunity to share my insights with an audience I believe can benefit immensely from online conversations and communities. Thank you to everyone at McGraw-Hill who worked with me to put this book together.

I also need to acknowledge my husband, Scott, for taking on without complaint the majority of the responsibilities around our house while I was writing this book, and thanks to my children, Brynn, Daniel, and Ryan, for not forgetting who I am while I'm in my office trying to meet deadlines. I still don't know how I got so lucky to have such an amazing husband and children. I also want to thank my family and friends who haven't disowned me despite my absence of late. I promise to come out of my writing hermit phase eventually. Thank you for waiting for me. Additionally, thank you to my parents, Bill and Carol Ann Henry, for baby-sitting my five-year-old triplets so I could have more time to write this book. They are very brave, very loved, and appreciated beyond words.

PART I

Get Started

The Who, What, and Why
of Social Media Marketing

Chapter 1

What Is Social Media Marketing?

There was a time, not so long ago, when the world of online marketing was one that small businesses didn't even consider joining. I remember my first job out of college in 1993, when I joined the marketing department within a division of AT&T (when AT&T was one of the biggest companies in the world). The division I worked for didn't even have a website at the time, and words like *blogs, Twitter, Facebook,* and *YouTube* didn't exist. Online marketing simply wasn't a strategic priority. Suffice it to say, a lot changed in less than two decades.

No longer is having a website a low-priority investment for large *or* small businesses. Today it's a necessity for survival. The biggest catalyst to getting businesses online came with the dawn of the 21st century, when a little thing called the social Web grew into the biggest marketing opportunity since television commercials made their debut. Soon businesses realized that being part of the social Web wasn't a fad that would fade away as fast as it had emerged. Instead, the businesses that *weren't* yet on the social Web scurried to claim their spaces and join the online conversation. Suddenly, building relationships took precedence over direct selling, with consumers, rather than companies, leading the way.

The social Web represents an amazing opportunity for *pull marketing* (defined in the sidebar "Pull vs. Push Marketing") that business leaders could never have dreamed of even 10 years ago. What business executive wouldn't salivate at the chance to have at his or her fin-

PULL VS. PUSH MARKETING

Pull marketing is generated by consumers who actively seek out, or ask for, information about products, services, and brands. The social Web offers businesses a pull marketing opportunity because consumer users actively engage businesses and "pull" more information from them, which ultimately leads to sales, brand building, and word-of-mouth buzz.

In contrast, push marketing is generated by businesses that actively "push" messages and information to consumers. Traditional marketing tactics such as advertising are perfect examples of push marketing: businesses feed messages to consumers with the hope that those messages will motivate consumers to take action and seek out products, services, and brands.

gertips an engaged audience of people who actively want to hear from that executive's company? The social Web makes that dream a reality. The trick for a small business owner is learning how to use the tools of the social Web to effectively build the business while still balancing all the other responsibilities of owning a small business. Believe it or not, it can be done—and quite successfully, as you'll learn from the many real-world success stories scattered throughout this book.

But before you can dive into the world of the social Web, you need to understand some of the terminology and jargon that go along with it. Before you continue reading, take some time to familiarize yourself with the definitions in the sidebar "Lessons in Social Web Lingo," so you can speak the language of the social Web and fully understand the concepts discussed in this book. Next, you need to understand exactly why all the fuss about the social Web is so important.

LESSONS IN SOCIAL WEB LINGO

Following are some of the most common terms and tools used in reference to the social Web. This list is not exhaustive but does introduce you to some of the most popular lingo and tools.

■ **Blog:** A website that includes frequently updated entries (posts) appearing in reverse chronological order and typically offering a comment feature where visitors can publish their opinions about the content they read on the blog.

- **Digg:** One of the most popular social bookmarking sites.

- **Facebook:** The most popular social networking site.

- **Flickr:** A popular website for uploading and sharing photos and other images.

- **Google Buzz:** A social networking tool available to users of Google Mail, or Gmail, Google's e-mail service.

- **LinkedIn:** A popular social networking site for businesspeople.

- **Microblogging:** Writing and publishing short entries (usually 140 characters or less) on social Web sites such as Twitter, Plurk, and Jaiku.

- **MySpace:** One of the earliest modern social networking sites; it is still popular but has been surpassed by Facebook in terms of usage.

- **SlideShare:** A website for uploading and sharing presentations.

- **Social bookmarking:** A method of saving and storing Web pages in a single online location for future use or for sharing with other Internet users. Sites such as Digg, StumbleUpon, Reddit, and Yahoo! Buzz provide social bookmarking capabilities.

- **Social networking:** Online networking that occurs through a variety of websites that allow users to share content, interact, and develop communities around similar interests. Examples include websites such as Facebook, LinkedIn, MySpace, Google Buzz, and Ning.

- **Social Web:** The second generation of the World Wide Web (Web 2.0), which focuses heavily on user-generated content, communities, networking, and social interaction.

- **StumbleUpon:** One of the most popular social bookmarking sites.

- **Twitter:** The most popular microblogging site.

- **YouTube:** The most popular website for uploading and sharing videos.

History of the World Wide Web

It took a long time for the World Wide Web to grow into an essential part of people's everyday lives. The Internet didn't truly become a household word until the 1990s, when dial-up modems and America Online were the go-to tools for businesses and individuals who wanted to check out the latest technology craze. At first, the World Wide Web was a navigational tool. Users could find information in a one-way communication stream. Most Web pages were text heavy and used rudimentary programming to display information in formats not much different from how information would be displayed on a printed page. In its infancy, the World Wide Web was interesting to many people but used by few.

Usage started to change when the Web moved from a strictly navigational tool to a transactional tool. Suddenly, people could make purchases, ask questions, get responses, and more all through the Internet. Websites were still primarily one-way communication tools, but visitors to those sites could perform actions that made their lives easier, thereby upping the interest level in the Web immensely. Sites like Amazon.com became popular quickly, and the Internet started to grow and evolve into a tool that more and more people embraced.

It didn't take long for people to demand faster access to the Web, and with the introduction of cable modems and high-speed Internet connections, the user base exploded. However, it wasn't until users found a way to join the world of online publishing that the Internet evolved from a transactional to a social tool. With the introduction of blogs, people found a way to publish online diaries and communicate with others in a two-way conversation. The Web evolved into a social medium, and user-generated content was born. The new generation of the Internet became known as Web 2.0 or the social Web.

When blogging applications like Blogger and WordPress, which require very little technical knowledge to use, hit the online scene, publishing user-generated content became easier than ever, and more and more people joined the online conversation for myriad reasons. Thanks to these free tools and the growing availability of high-speed Internet access at affordable prices (no longer did people have to pay per hour of use, as flat monthly fees became the norm), the barriers to entry to the social Web were shattered. Anyone was welcome to the party, and the party grew and grew.

Blogs became far more than personal diaries. They were transformed into an important source of information from authoritative influencers, and businesses started to take notice. As sites like MySpace and Facebook made it even easier and more entertaining to connect with people via the social Web, the online conversation grew louder and reached even further. By the time Twitter made its value known in 2008, the world had already gotten much smaller. Suddenly, more people around the world had access to more information in a timelier manner, and life would never be the same.

The Social Web Delivers Information Across Borders Anytime

One of the first global stories that proved the reach and influence of the social Web came out of Iran and was delivered to the world not by experts but by everyday people via Twitter. In June 2009, citizens of Iran protested following a questionable presidential election process. News out of the country was halted, and the rest of the world waited with bated breath to hear what happened in the fallout from the criticized election. The world didn't have to wait long as individual Iranian citizens found their way to their computers and began sending 140-character updates through their Twitter profiles to share the story happening on the streets as Iranians protested against the powers that be.

What made the story of the 2009 Iranian presidential election more poignant is the fact that Twitter became not just *a* communications tool during the aftermath but rather *the* communications tool. Its influence was so important that the U.S. State Department contacted the Twitter team shortly after the election protests began and requested that a scheduled Twitter maintenance that would take the site offline temporarily be postponed so communications could continue to flow out of Iran. You can read more about the social Web's role in the Iran election protest in the sidebar "Social Media and the 2009 Iranian Presidential Election Protests."

The global reach and influence of Twitter and blogs was demonstrated again in June 2009 with the news of performer Michael Jackson's death. That news broke not through a traditional news source but on an entertainment blog, TMZ (www.tmz.com). It took hours for traditional news sources to report what had already been announced on the TMZ blog. Immediately after TMZ broke the news, people around the world began talking about it on Twitter, ultimately causing the microblogging site to crash due to a massive amount of traffic.

In fact, this would become a common occurrence in 2009 and 2010 when people around the world turned to Twitter again and again to discuss and learn about high-profile current events.

If anyone thought Twitter or the tools of the social Web were meaningless, their opinions likely changed in June 2009. The social Web was here to stay, and it had become an integral part of society, politics, business, culture, entertainment, and more. In other words, the social Web permeated all areas of life around the globe, and in 2009, the world recognized its power. Businesses that hadn't been active on the social Web before would need to get active soon, or they would be left behind.

By 2010, the social Web became mainstream. Hundreds of millions of people had Facebook profiles, and Twitter delivered a billion tweets per hour. When a massive earthquake struck Haiti on January

SOCIAL MEDIA AND THE 2009 IRANIAN PRESIDENTIAL ELECTION PROTESTS

On June 12, 2009, Iran held its presidential election, and Mahmoud Ahmadinejad beat Mir-Hossein Mousavi by a substantial margin. Mousavi's camp warned Iranians of possible voter fraud, which quickly erupted into protests in the streets of Iran, but first, people took to the social Web to share their opinions. Within hours, people from inside and outside of Iran were talking about the election scandal on Twitter, uploading photos from the streets to Flickr and Twitter, and uploading videos to YouTube. One of those Twitter accounts, @Change_for_Iran, was purported to be owned by an Iranian student who shared information from the streets where student protests were reported to grow to groups of tens of thousands.

Just three days after the election, a recount of votes began, and green became the official color of the opposition movement. People began to "green" their Twitter avatars (the personal images that appear in the upper left corner of all Twitter profiles), and during the week of June 15, 2009, Twitter users adopted hashtags (keywords preceded by the # symbol, used to help people follow updates related to topics of interest on Twitter) such as #iranelection to follow the events occurring in Iran.

Word spread via the social Web that the Iranian government was restricting journalists' access to events and limiting access to the Internet so Iranian citizens couldn't share or read all information from outside

12, 2010, Twitter and the tools of the social Web became more than just methods for sharing information. Suddenly, they became lifelines.

Twitter profiles and Facebook groups were created allowing people to publish information about loved ones they couldn't contact, and millions of dollars in donations were collected through people joining together in support of Haitian citizens, using Twitter hashtags to ensure people around the world knew what was happening in the ravaged country. Again, the sheer volume of traffic to Twitter caused the site to go down temporarily. Images of the aftermath taken by survivors were uploaded and shared on sites like Twitter, Flickr, and Facebook, and videos of the destruction, rescues, and relief operations showed the world how people could come together to help a nation in need. Once again, the power of the social Web crossed borders and influenced the world. The social Web was here to stay, and no one wanted to be left out of the global conversation.

the country. The Iranian powers-that-be limited citizens' access to Twitter as well. Suddenly, Twitter was filled with posts sharing information about how Iranians could get around those government restrictions and access the site. In fact, Twitter became a vital communications channel, and on June 15, 2009, the U.S. State Department contacted the Twitter team to request that scheduled maintenance be postponed to ensure communications continued to flow out of Iran. Twitter cofounder Biz Stone wrote an article, published in the *Times* of London, England (TimesOnline.co.uk), detailing this event and how Twitter and the world changed in 2009. This insightful piece is reprinted in Appendix A.

By the weekend of June 19, 2009, violence had erupted in Iran, and photos and videos began flooding Twitter, Flickr, Facebook, and YouTube. Most of the videos were captured by amateurs and protesters, and the shocking images spread virally across the social Web. The election results stood, but the story of the 2009 Iranian presidential election had the opportunity to be heard around the globe thanks largely to the individuals and the tools of the social Web. Citizen journalism took center stage during a difficult time in history and gave people around the world access to uncensored (albeit unverified) information that is unlikely to have spread without the social Web.

Business Embraces Social Media Marketing

The first decade of the 21st century can be remembered as a time when businesses were wary of and confused by the social Web, but the second decade of the 21st century marks a time when businesses need to embrace the social Web and make it an integral part of their strategic marketing plans. That means large and small businesses should not only be present on the social Web, but also have a defined social media marketing strategy. Let's take a step backward and define social media and social media marketing:

> Social media *are the online publishing and communications tools, sites, and destinations of Web 2.0 that are rooted in conversations, engagement, and participation.*
>
> Social media marketing *is any form of direct or indirect marketing that is used to build awareness, recognition, recall, and action for a brand, business, product, person, or other entity and is carried out using the tools of the social Web, such as blogging, microblogging, social networking, social bookmarking, and content sharing.*

Social media marketing can include specific tactics such as sharing a coupon or announcing a sale on Facebook or Twitter, or it could include broader brand-building initiatives like communicating with people on LinkedIn or creating interesting content on a blog, in a video uploaded to YouTube, or in a presentation shared on SlideShare. Since social media marketing is still evolving, there is no written set of guidelines you can follow, but that's also what makes it so open, interesting, and fun.

The key word in "social Web" and "social media marketing" is *social*. As long as you're contributing to the conversation that's happening on the social Web, you're doing it right. It may seem overwhelming and intimidating, but as with any form of communication and networking, once you try it, you might learn that you really like it. Remember when using e-mail involved a huge learning curve? Today, using e-mail is not just second nature, but also something most people couldn't live without. Once you join the conversation on the social Web, you'll learn that it can become second nature, just as e-mail is to you today.

The Disruption of Interruption Marketing

Critical to your business's success on the social Web is your understanding of social media marketing as being very different from traditional marketing. While some people refer to social media marketing as "interruption marketing," I argue that social media marketing is exactly the opposite of interruption marketing. Rather than causing consumers to *stop* what they're doing, effective social media marketing *enhances* what they're already doing. While a television commercial *interrupts* the program a person is watching, effective social media marketing should make a person's activities more interesting or better.

For example, when you share amazing, relevant content in a conversation taking place among your social Web connections, you add value to that conversation rather than interrupting it. Traditional marketing is intended to stop consumers in their tracks, but effective social media marketing should encourage those consumers to continue on their original paths armed with more knowledge, support, or confidence than they had before.

With that in mind, social media marketing has disrupted marketers' long-held theories related to selling products and building businesses. Instead of just catching the attention of consumers in order to deliver a message and provoke a response, effective social media marketing requires listening, understanding, and participation to add value and build relationships without interrupting. In short, social media marketing has disrupted traditional marketing, causing a fundamental shift in strategic marketing planning and tactical execution, and it has helped to level the business playing field as both small and large businesses (and every business in between) can join the conversation with few barriers to entry. Even if you have just a little bit of time, the social Web audience can be yours.

Chapter 2

Why Are Businesses Using Social Media Marketing?

Now that you have an understanding of what the social Web is and some of the commonly used tools of the social Web, it's time to learn why businesses are using them. The most important thing you can learn from reading this book is the potential of using social media:

> *Social media marketing offers the single largest opportunity for entre-preneurs, small businesses, midsize companies, and large corpora-tions to build their brands and their businesses.*

Don't believe it? There are countless examples of companies of all sizes leveraging the tools of the social Web to grow their businesses. One such example comes from a woman named Cindy Gordon, who led the marketing effort for Universal Orlando Resort in 2008 to announce and create excitement around the new Wizarding World of Harry Potter theme park destination.

In 2007, the executives at Universal told Gordon that her objective was to raise awareness of the new theme park attraction, and she was given a sizable budget to make it happen. However, instead of invest-ing millions of dollars in Super Bowl commercials, Gordon turned to the social Web to spread the word about the Wizarding World of Harry Potter. She invited the top seven Harry Potter bloggers to a midnight webcast (an online broadcast of multimedia content such as audio or video) held on May 31, 2007, when they were told they'd be the first to hear some exciting news. During the webcast, Gordon announced that the Wizarding World of Harry Potter was coming. Those seven people blogged about the new theme park, with posts going live on fan blogs as early as 12:02 A.M., just two minutes after the webcast began. Within 24 hours, by Universal's estimates, 350 million people around the world heard the news about the Wizarding World of Harry Potter theme park—all from Gordon telling just seven people.

You could argue that Gordon's story doesn't apply to small business owners who lack the global brand recognition that the Harry Potter series of books and movies already enjoyed at the time Universal announced the Wizarding World of Harry Potter, but the fundamental reasons that social media marketing works truly do apply to businesses of all sizes. In short, it's about getting access to people. Businesses don't hesitate to invest money in commercials and direct mail in an attempt to drive a few people into their brick-and-mortar locations, where they can stand in front of those consumers for a few minutes and convey the benefits of buying from them. However, the idea of investing almost no money and directly communicating with a huge audience of engaged individuals across the social Web still doesn't make sense to many business owners. If that's not a missed opportunity, then I don't know what is.

Think of it this way: when you need to find information about a product, service, brand, or business, where do you look for that information? The vast majority of consumers turn to Google (or their preferred search engine). Your business had better be represented in the search results related to your products and services, or you're likely to lose a lot of potential customers. But how do you boost your business's search engine rankings? Of course, using search engine optimization (SEO) techniques to increase your search rankings for your targeted keywords is important, but there is more that you can do than focusing on keywords. The social Web offers a multitude of opportunities for you to increase your business's search rankings.

For example, consider what I refer to as the compounding effect of blogging. Imagine you're a small business owner who writes a blog. While your business's website might include only 10 pages (so that's all search engines can index), a blog offers a new entry point and a new opportunity for search engines to find you with each new blog post you publish. If you publish a blog post every day for a year, that equates to 365 more entry points to your website (via your blog). That's a lot of ways for a search engine to find you. Search engines like Google also index Twitter updates and other social networking content, which offer even more ways for you to be found via search.

But that's not all. If you publish amazing content, then other bloggers, Twitter users, and so on will take notice. They're likely to link to your amazing content and share it with others. Each new link to your website or blog increases your search rankings, because search engines like Google rank search results by using algorithms that rely heavily on the number of incoming links to a site. The theory is that sites with a lot of incoming links (particularly from authoritative websites) must include great information, or no one would link to them. Therefore, results for those sites are ranked higher than results for sites with fewer incoming links. Leveraging the compounding effect of blogging is just one more way that the tools of the social Web can help you build your business—by increasing traffic to your website.

How Social Media Marketing Can Help Your Business

Consumers have more options than ever, thanks to the ease of finding information online, and brands and businesses get more exposure than ever, thanks to the social Web. It's an incredible marketing channel that allows businesses to achieve a variety of marketing goals. In Part III of this book, you can learn more about how social media marketing can help your business in much greater detail, but as an introduction, following are five of the most common goals of social media marketing:

1. **Relationship building:** The primary benefit of social media marketing is the ability to build relationships with actively engaged consumers, online influencers, peers, and more.
2. **Brand building:** Social media conversations present the perfect way to raise brand awareness, boost brand recognition and recall, and increase brand loyalty.

3. **Publicity:** Social media marketing provides an outlet where businesses can share important information and modify negative perceptions.

4. **Promotions:** Through social media marketing, you can provide exclusive discounts and opportunities to your audience in order to make these people feel valued and special, as well as to meet short-term goals.

5. **Market research:** You can use the tools of the social Web to learn about your customers, create demographic and behavioral profiles of your customers, find niche audiences, learn about consumers' wants and needs, and learn about competitors.

While social media marketing should be viewed very much as a long-term marketing strategy, you can use it for short-term marketing pushes through promotions (as described in the fourth goal). Some businesses have a lot of success using social media marketing for short-term boosts in business, but remember, you need to build relationships and an audience on the social Web before you can have any expectations for positive short-term promotional results. In other words, social media marketing success is a multistep process.

The Four Pillars of Social Media Marketing

The tools of the social Web offer a unique opportunity for marketing businesses, products, and services that didn't exist a decade ago. The marketing landscape is continually evolving, and we're only at the beginning of the social media marketing story. It's an exciting time for marketers and business owners, but it can also be an intimidating and challenging time, simply because the path to success in social media marketing has yet to be carved out for everyone to follow. Today, each business must experiment and adjust its social media marketing tactics in order to find the best mix to meet its goals. The key to successfully marketing your business on the social Web is to set your fears aside and dive in, but before you do so, you need to fully understand the fundamentals that apply to any social media marketing strategy.

Earlier in this chapter, you learned how social media marketing can help build your brand, directly promote your business, provide publicity, and so on, but at the core of any social media marketing plan stand the four pillars of social media marketing: read, create, share, and discuss. If you don't fully understand the four pillars of social media marketing, then your strategies and tactics will be unfocused, haphazard, and ineffective. In other words, just as when you're building a house you need to build a solid foundation and continually maintain that foundation before you can build your structure and start living in it, developing and implementing a social media marketing plan is a long-term strategy that requires persistence and patience in order to achieve success. That strategy can be enhanced with short-term tactics, but taking care of the foundation never goes away.

For success in social media marketing, you must review the four pillars of social media marketing and commit to including all four in your social media marketing activities at all times.

Pillar One: Read

A successful social media marketing plan begins with research, and that research must be ongoing. In simplest terms, social media marketing requires a lot of reading. Not only must you stay current on what's going on in your industry, but you also need to be aware of the ongoing online conversations happening that are related to your industry, business, products, services, customers, and competitors. Earlier in this chapter, you learned how social media marketing can be used for relationship building with your peers, industry leaders, and customers. Without reading and staying current and knowledgeable, it's nearly impossible to effectively create, share, and discuss—the next three pillars of social media marketing.

Reading can happen in a variety of forms. You should digest as much information related to your business as possible daily, so you can effectively communicate with your audience honestly and intelligently. The sidebar "10 Media You Should Read as Part of Your Social Media Marketing Plan" suggests media to read daily as part of your 30-minutes-a-day social media marketing plan.

QUICK TIP

To stay current on news and information about your business online, sign up for Google Alerts (www.google .com/alerts). Enter your keywords of choice into the Google Alerts online form, and provide your e-mail address. An e-mail is automatically sent to you anytime Google finds new relevant content.

10 MEDIA YOU SHOULD READ AS PART OF YOUR SOCIAL MEDIA MARKETING PLAN

The best social media marketers are well versed on their industries, competitors, customers, trends, and all other topics related to their businesses. Following are suggested traditional and new media that you should read continually as an essential first step in developing an effective social media marketing plan:

1. Industry websites
2. Industry news sites
3. Industry press releases
4. Blogs that relate to your business directly or indirectly, written by industry experts, companies, consumers, and more
5. E-books
6. Industry periodicals (online and offline)
7. Twitter feeds by prominent people in your industry
8. Online videos published by individuals or groups related to your industry
9. Podcasts and online radio shows produced by individuals or groups related to your industry
10. Printed newspapers and periodicals (they're not dead yet!)

Pillar Two: Create

Most social media experts suggest that creating great content is the most important part of any social media marketing plan, and I absolutely agree with that claim. In Chapter 3, you'll learn more about the fundamental rule for leveraging social media for marketing purposes: adding value. For now, believe me when I tell you that your efforts at social media marketing are for naught if you're not creating and publishing useful and meaningful content online.

Success in social media marketing comes from developing online conversations about your business, brand, products, and promotions. It's hard to start those conversations, sustain them, and motivate others to share them if you're not offering content that interests your target audience. Keep in mind, creating amazing content goes deeper than sharing useful snippets such as coupon codes and discount announcements. Amazing content truly adds value to the audience and the online conversation. For tips on writing amazing social media

FIVE TIPS FOR WRITING AMAZING SOCIAL MEDIA CONTENT

Follow these suggestions to ensure that the social media content you deliver really is amazing from the audience's viewpoint:

1. Amazing content is written in your own voice, making it personable.
2. Amazing content is written using the same language and tone in which you speak to your target audience while maintaining the level of professionalism that matches your target audience's expectations.
3. Amazing content is published consistently. Don't publish content and then disappear, or your audience will disappear, too.
4. Amazing content is devoid of corporate rhetoric and jargon that confuses the target audience.
5. Amazing content is transparent, meaning the target audience views it as open, honest, reliable, and trustworthy.

content, check out the sidebar "Five Tips for Writing Amazing Social Media Content."

Pillar Three: Share

A unique aspect of social media marketing is sharing content as a method to indirectly market a business. When most people think about marketing, they think of direct advertising and promotional methods. However, social media marketing adds new elements to the marketing mix based on behaviors related to sharing. In a world that has become somewhat cynical and distrusting of advertising, consumers have come to depend more than ever on relationships, reviews, recommendations, and conversations. You can leverage that desire for sharing information by sharing content online. In essence, the social Web brought behavioral targeting to the forefront of marketing strategy after decades of reliance on demographic targeting.

Sharing content can come in two primary forms. First, you can share interesting and useful content you find online during your reading (the first pillar). Whether you find a great blog post filled with tips that could help your customers use products like the ones you sell or you find a timely online news article that discusses changes coming in your industry, you can share that content online and indirectly boost your social media presence, which in turn indirectly markets

10 POPULAR WEBSITES FOR SHARING CONTENT

1. Digg (http://digg.com)
2. StumbleUpon (www.stumbleupon.com)
3. Reddit (www.reddit.com)
4. Twitter (http://twitter.com)
5. Facebook (www.facebook.com)
6. LinkedIn (www.linkedin.com)
7. Flickr (www.flickr.com)
8. Picasa Web Albums (http://picasa.google.com/features.html)
9. YouTube (www.youtube.com)
10. SlideShare (www.slideshare.net)

your business. You can share content with consumers, peers, industry experts, and others. In other words, there is not just one type of content you can share, nor is there a single audience with whom you can share that content. Just as you use different traditional marketing tactics and messages to promote your business to different segments of your customer audience, so you should share different types of content with applicable segments of your online audience.

In addition, you can share content that you created (the second pillar). For example, you can upload presentations through Slide-Share, videos on YouTube, and pictures on Flickr. You can also share your own content that you publish online through different social media tools. If you publish a blog post that you believe is useful, you can share it via Twitter, via social bookmarking, through your social networking profiles, and more. The goal is to get out the word about your content to a wider audience. Fortunately, the tools of the social Web make it very easy to do exactly that. These tools and more are discussed in detail in Part II, but a list of some of the most popular websites for sharing content appears in the sidebar "10 Popular Websites for Sharing Content."

Pillar Four: Discuss

As you create and share more and more amazing content, your online audience will grow organically. In time, many members of that audience will become your loyal followers. The more you engage them by creating and sharing amazing content, the more they are likely to vocalize their appreciation, thoughts, and opinions (both positive and negative). The final pillar of social media marketing is discussion. When your audience interacts with you by leaving a comment on one of your blog posts, sharing *your* content, connecting with you via Twitter or social networking, and so on, it is essential that you respond to them. No one likes to be ignored, but everyone likes to be acknowledged positively.

In other words, show your audience members that you appreciate them, respect their opinions, and want to build relationships with them. Think of it this way: Would you ignore someone who walked up to you in person and started talking to you? We all know the polite thing to do is to respond to that person, and just as you wouldn't ignore someone in person, you shouldn't ignore him or her online.

The power of social media marketing comes from your loyal audience members, who often become your vocal brand advocates and brand guardians. Their collective voices can champion your brand and your messages by sharing your content across the social Web, and they can protect your brand by speaking out against negative and false information. It's this power that has caused the Internet to evolve from a navigational and transactional destination to an audience-centric destination offering immense opportunity for word-of-mouth marketing.

QUICK TIP

Aim to publish amazing content that is *share-worthy*, meaning people will find it useful enough to share it with their own audiences.

Many of the most popular social media experts claim that their success came primarily from building loyal followings, which started by creating great content but grew because they responded to all comments left on their blogs, social networking interactions, and Twitter interactions. They also answered all e-mails and made themselves accessible to their audiences by showing audience members they were valued. For a perfect example, see "How Gary Vaynerchuk Used Social Media to Create a Multimillion-Dollar Wine Business."

While this pillar of social media marketing doesn't require a monetary investment (unless you hire someone to do it for you), it is time consuming, particularly as your online presence grows. However, the rewards can be exponentially more powerful than other marketing initiatives that require significant monetary investments.

HOW GARY VAYNERCHUK USED SOCIAL MEDIA TO CREATE A MULTIMILLION-DOLLAR WINE BUSINESS

Gary Vaynerchuk grew up working in his father's Springfield, New Jersey, wine store. He had a love of wines from an early age, and that interest turned into a visible passion. Gary discovered blogs and online video and asked his father if he could start a blog and online video program for the store. His father indulged him, and Gary began publishing interesting content that showed off his contagious passion for wine. Word spread quickly, and his *Wine Library TV* video audiences grew around the world.

Gary credits much of his success to the fact that he actively engages with his audience. He responds to every e-mail he gets and spends far more time interacting with people via the social Web than he spends promoting his business. In fact, Gary has been quoted saying that for every hour he spends promoting on the social Web, he spends another three hours interacting. He truly understands how to use the social Web to grow a business, and that's why he has been so successful with it.

Today, Gary's wine store has sales of $50 million per year, with over half of all sales coming from the Internet. He is a sought-after social media consultant and speaker and signed a multimillion-dollar deal to write multiple books in which he shares his knowledge and experience using the tools of the social Web to build a business. Nearly a million people follow him on Twitter, and he is a celebrity in the world of social media marketing. And it all started with a small business blog.

By following the suggestions provided throughout this book and the sample 30-minutes-a-day social media marketing plans in Chapter 22, you'll learn how to balance your daily online activities within the four pillars of social media marketing to find the right mix for you that will help you achieve your goals.

Chapter 3

Who Is Doing It Right and Wrong?

As you join the world of the social Web with business goals in mind, it's essential to remember there are not yet best practices related to social media marketing. New media presents a new marketing opportunity. Consider how long advertising has been around, and still, there are many opinions about what works and what doesn't in advertising. The same is true for social media marketing, and I expect the path to success won't be clear to businesses and marketers for many years to come. Let's face it—we're just figuring out what works in e-mail marketing, and its importance is already fading.

Regardless of how you spend your time on the social Web in an attempt to grow your business, you can count on one fundamental rule: you must add value. Adding value starts by listening before you join the online conversation. In other words, your social media marketing efforts should not be dominated by self-promotion. As mentioned in Chapter 2 in the telling of Gary Vaynerchuk's social media marketing success story, you must spend far less time self-promoting on the social Web and far more time interacting and building relationships.

Social Media Marketing and the 80-20 Rule

An easy way to balance the amount of self-promotion you do on the social Web for your business versus the amount of interacting you do is to follow the 80-20 rule of marketing. Spend 80 percent of your time on the social Web interacting and 20 percent of your time self-promoting. You can apply the 80-20 rule regardless of how much time you spend on the social Web each day. Whether you're spending one hour or five hours on social media marketing on any given day, divide your efforts during that time using the 80-20 rule. This process helps to prevent you from overpromoting and annoying your audience on the social Web.

Think of it this way: If you meet someone at a party, and all that person does is talk about herself during your conversation, then you'll probably look for any excuse to extricate yourself from that conversation and actively avoid her in the future. However, if you meet a person at a party and the person asks a multitude of questions about you, making you the star of the conversation, then you're far more likely to want to continue talking to her. The same holds true for your social media conversations. Don't bore your audience with your own story. Instead, get involved in audience members' stories. Listen and then add valuable content. This is how relationships are built on the social Web.

The Value of Earned Media and Manufactured Word-of-Mouth Advertising

As you build more and more relationships with people across the social Web, they'll come to have expectations for what you'll bring to the table during any given interaction. Therefore, you need to consistently and persistently engage your audience. Provide useful information that helps or entertains your audience, so audience members will want to share with their own connections across the social Web. Your engaged social media audience can turn into a network of your most loyal brand advocates.

You can *earn* media coverage via the social Web by building relationships with people who become your band of brand advocates.

They'll share your content, help promote your business, talk about you, and defend you against naysayers. In essence, through social media, you can manufacture word-of-mouth marketing. Earned media is one of the most powerful forms of publicity because studies show that consumers trust other people (even strangers) more than they trust any form of marketing.

According to a study conducted by Nielsen Online in July 2009, 92 percent of Internet users in North America trust recommendations from people they know, and 72 percent trust consumer opinions posted online, with all forms of traditional marketing deemed less trustworthy. For example, only 61 percent of the study participants trust ads on television or radio, and only 53 percent trust billboards or outdoor advertising. Therefore, the opinions of bloggers, micro-bloggers, social networking connections, and so on can have a demonstrated effect on your business's success. Take the time to get to know your online audience and build relationships with audience members, so you can earn some of that media for your business.

The Evolution of *Consumers* to *Prosumers*

With the expansion of the social Web, people moved from being *consumers* to *prosumers*. Rather than simply consuming products, people on the social Web have become influential voices of those products. They can have a significant impact on the success or failure of businesses, products, services, and brands through their social Web participation. The challenge for businesses is finding the prosumers within their industry niche, connecting with them, building relationships with them, and giving them valuable information that they want to share with their own audiences.

Knowing the potential power and influence of prosumers, it's critical that you not only allow them to have access to your valuable content and messages but also allow them to share your content and messages. To truly build your social Web presence and build your business, you need to remove all barriers to viewing and sharing your online content. Five years ago, capturing e-mail addresses was a top priority, and any exclusive information offered online required a person to complete a registration form or provide an e-mail address to access it. With the growth of the social Web, that line of thinking

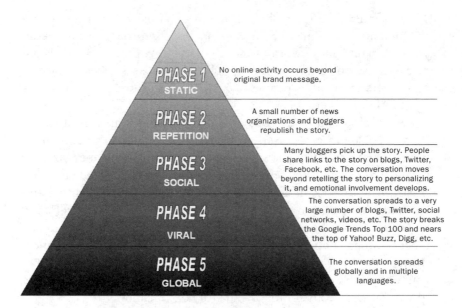

PHASE 1 STATIC	No online activity occurs beyond original brand message.
PHASE 2 REPETITION	A small number of news organizations and bloggers republish the story.
PHASE 3 SOCIAL	Many bloggers pick up the story. People share links to the story on blogs, Twitter, Facebook, etc. The conversation moves beyond retelling the story to personalizing it, and emotional involvement develops.
PHASE 4 VIRAL	The conversation spreads to a very large number of blogs, Twitter, social networks, videos, etc. The story breaks the Google Trends Top 100 and nears the top of Yahoo! Buzz, Digg, etc.
PHASE 5 GLOBAL	The conversation spreads globally and in multiple languages.

Figure 3.1   Five phases of viral marketing

has changed. Removing all barriers to your best content and letting it flow across the Web through social sharing and discussions gives your brand and business greater opportunities for success than stockpiling e-mail addresses can deliver. Furthermore, removing barriers opens the door to your content going viral.

Viral marketing should not be confused with social media marketing. As shown in Figure 3.1, viral marketing is an extension of social media marketing. It's the result of massive sharing and the organic spreading of your content across the Internet. When your band of loyal brand advocates and prosumers begins sharing your content, you can pat yourself on the back and feel confident you've harnessed an amazing opportunity. However, when your content spreads beyond that evangelist audience to a massive audience of Web users around the world (phases 4 and 5), you've hit the viral marketing jackpot.

Find and Own Your Audience

Your social media marketing strategy should be focused and dedicated to making sure you *own* your audience in your niche or online space. Unlike traditional advertising, where you're attempting to steal precious moments in time with consumers, you truly can own an audience through social media marketing. Even large corporations are realizing the potential that owning your audience can deliver in terms of results. For example, in 2010, PepsiCo shifted millions of dollars away from placing ads in the Super Bowl broadcast, as the company had done for years, and moved that money to social media marketing with the successful Pepsi Refresh Project.

However, you can't own an audience until you find people online. Interestingly, 2008 marked the first year that people spent more time on the social Web than they did reading and sending e-mail. Every business can find members of its target audience on the social Web. Even the Salvation Army has found an opportunity on the social Web, with Facebook pages offering virtual red kettles to accept donations from people who become fans of those pages.

Invest your energy in searching for your best audience on the social Web. Where are the people you want to reach hanging out online? Once you find them, spend some time there with them. Join the conversation, offer useful information, and make your mark as a valued, engaging connection. Only then can you lead people to your own amazing content on your blog, Twitter profile, and so on—your branded destinations.

Successful social media marketing is rooted in relationships. While your online presence will certainly grow organically over time as you publish more and more great content, traffic doesn't adhere to the saying "If you build it, they will come." You need to find your audience and then give those people a reason to want to follow you again and again and again. Check out Chapter 4 for more steps toward success in social media marketing.

Who's Doing It Wrong?

Before you begin your foray into the world of the social Web, it's important to heed the lessons learned by companies before you. There are many examples of businesses that have gotten it wrong when it comes to effectively connecting with the online audience. Take some time to familiarize yourself with these stories and learn from them so that you don't make the same mistakes.

The Dell Debacle

One of the best examples of social media marketing gone wrong comes from Dell, whose foray into the social Web came with very public embarrassment. On June 14, 2007, a former employee who worked in a Dell retail kiosk sent a list titled "22 Confessions of a Former Dell Sales Manager" to one of the most popular blogs, *The Consumerist*. *The Consumerist* published the list, which disclosed secrets about warranty programs, tips for getting discounts, and much more. One day later, the blog received an e-mail from Dell, demanding that the article be removed from the site. Nine hours later, the article had not been removed, and Dell sent a second letter demanding that the post be taken down, with mention of getting legal counsel involved in the matter if *The Consumerist* did not comply.

Understanding the power of the social Web and Dell's obvious misunderstanding of how the social Web works, *The Consumerist* published both e-mails from Dell, as well as the pointed e-mail that *The Consumerist*'s team sent to Dell in response. In less than 48 hours, the two posts had been shared more than 5,000 times and received hundreds of comments. Bloggers from around the world picked up the story, including some of the most popular bloggers at the time like Jeff Jarvis of *BuzzMachine*. This was a time before rampant use of Twitter and Facebook, so one can only imagine how much further the story could have spread if these additional tools had been more popular.

On June 16, 2007, just two days after the "22 Confessions" post was published by *The Consumerist*, Dell realized the error of its ways. The company learned the hard way that trying to stop the online conversation from happening on the social Web is a huge mistake. In an effort to clean up, Dell posted its own response to the "22 Confessions" article, which the company called "Dell's 23 Confessions," on its own Direct2Dell blog. The post began by saying, "Now's not the time to mince words, so let me just say it . . . we blew it." The post ended with these words: "No matter where we are at any point in time, there's always room for improvement. The key to our success in these areas depends squarely on opening the lines of communications with our customers, taking some time to assess what the feedback means, and taking action on that feedback. We'll keep doing that and think we'll ultimately be a better company for it." It took time for Dell to truly learn to walk the walk, but June of 2007 marked a turning point for Dell and many other companies in terms of how they viewed the importance of the social Web in building their businesses.

By 2009, Dell had embraced one of the most important elements of successful social media marketing: effectively surrounding consumers with these and other branded Dell experiences from which they could self-select how they wanted to interact with the brand. Dell now has a brand presence in a variety of social Web locations:

- Dell operates several successful Twitter profiles.
- Dell runs a number of blogs, including the Direct2Dell blog for consumers.
- Dell owns the Dell Community social network for consumers.
- Dell is on Facebook and LinkedIn.
- Dell has an active online forum.
- Dell has a presence on Flickr.
- Dell has its own YouTube channel.

Some of Dell's most successful social media marketing efforts are the company's Twitter profiles. For example, the @DellOutlet Twitter profile, which offers updates on special discounts and sales available on Dell equipment, had 1.5 million followers and was responsible for $3 million in business within just two years. The @DellnoBrasil account generated $800,000 in its first eight months, demonstrating the reach and influence of social media around the world. In December 2009, Dell reported having between 100 and 200 employees using Twitter in some capacity and over 3.5 million connections via its main social networks and profiles on sites like Facebook, Twitter, Flickr, and YouTube. That's a big leap from trying to stop the online conversation just two years earlier.

United Airlines Breaks Guitars

As the preceding story from Dell tells us, trying to control the conversation on the social Web by sending cease-and-desist letters and asking bloggers to take down posts that cast a brand in a negative light can lead to more harm than good. Similarly, *not* responding to negativity on the social Web can damage a business. United Airlines learned this lesson the hard way in 2009 when a series of YouTube videos called "United Breaks Guitars" started making their way across the social Web.

In spring 2008, musician David Carroll took a United Airlines flight on his way to a one-week tour. Due to new carry-on baggage restrictions, Carroll was forced to check his $3,500 Taylor guitar.

While he sat in the plane on the tarmac, another passenger brought everyone's attention to the United Airlines baggage handlers who were throwing baggage, including Carroll's guitar, into the plane with little care for whether or not the items made it to their final destination in one piece. When Carroll was reunited with his guitar at his destination, it was severely damaged. After nine months of phone calls and discussions with dozens of United Airlines employees, Carroll was finally told that United Airlines would not compensate him for his damaged guitar. That was United Airlines' first mistake.

Carroll decided that if United Airlines wouldn't compensate him, then he wanted to warn other people about the lack of customer service he had experienced, so others wouldn't suffer the same fate. He recorded a song and video called "United Breaks Guitars," which told his story in an entertaining manner. He uploaded his video (which turned into a series of videos as the story progressed) on July 9, 2009, and in just over two months, 5.3 million people had viewed it. The video spread across the social Web faster than Carroll could have imagined. Traditional news sources picked up the story, and even Bob Taylor of Taylor Guitars got involved and uploaded his own YouTube video on July 10, 2009, offering his support to Carroll.

United Airlines recognized the power of the social Web quickly as Carroll's first video went viral almost immediately. United Airlines finally took the initiative and contacted Carroll, offering to compensate him for the damage done to his guitar. Carroll declined the money on principle and asked United Airlines to donate it to charity. On July 10, 2009, he uploaded a new video to YouTube in which he explained his conversation with United Airlines, and on August 17, 2009, he uploaded the second original song and video in his "United Breaks Guitars" series, which received over 300,000 views within two weeks. By March 2010, Carroll's videos were viewed on YouTube by just under 10 million people.

The lesson to learn from United Airlines' error is twofold. First, you need to monitor what's being said about your business on the social Web, as discussed in Chapter 1, and second, you must have a plan in place to handle negativity on the social Web before it's too late. While it's possible to ignore much of the negative comments made about your business on the social Web, you need to stay on top of the online conversation, so you can massage perceptions and nudge conversations in the right direction when necessary. You can learn more about the social Web and negative publicity in Chapter 5, so you don't make the same mistake that United Airlines did.

Who's Doing It Right?

An essential part of developing your own social media marketing strategy is benchmarking companies that truly get how the social Web community works and are doing it right. While other companies' strategies won't always be right for your business, there are lessons to learn from all of the positive examples of companies leveraging the tools of the social Web to grow.

Comcast Cares

Comcast uses the tools of the social Web a bit differently than Dell does but has achieved its own success in the world of social media marketing using Twitter. The @ComcastCares Twitter profile is managed by Frank Eliason, the director of national customer service operations for Comcast and leader of the Comcast Digital Care Team. Comcast paved the way for using Twitter as a direct customer service tool and an indirect marketing tool. Frank mixes the @ComcastCares Twitter updates between personal snippets that make the Twitter stream human and responses to customer service questions that add value. Instead of trying to hide customer service questions and problems, Comcast openly discusses them through the @ComcastCares Twitter stream, which helps build the brand image as honest, open, and accessible.

Zappos Dares

Zappos is another company with a strong presence on the social Web. You can find Zappos on YouTube, multiple blogs, and more. Even former Zappos CEO Tony Hsieh got involved on Twitter. His @Zappos Twitter profile was filled with useful information as well as personal updates and pictures that were interesting or just fun. The @Zappos Twitter stream is still a perfect example of adding personality to a business social media presence. If you're too boring, no one will want to follow you. Zappos clearly understands that.

Whole Foods Is Everywhere

Whole Foods does an excellent job of surrounding consumers with branded experiences across the social Web. The company has dozens of Twitter profiles (each store has its own Twitter profile), blogs, a YouTube channel, podcasts, a Facebook page, a Flickr photo profile, and more. Each profile offers valuable content and conversation, which gives the Whole Foods brand a personality and a direct dialogue with consumers. Whole Foods has been very successful at building relationships with consumers via the social Web, which leads to trust, brand advocacy, and earned media.

Small Business Trumps Big Business on the Social Web

Certainly, many well-known brands and companies are having success with social media marketing, but that's not to say small business owners aren't doing just as well, albeit on a smaller scale. In fact, I'd argue that small businesses have a bigger opportunity to build their businesses via social media marketing than big businesses do, simply because they can move faster, get closer to consumers, and make decisions in a more timely fashion. While big businesses have deeper pockets, that's not necessarily important when it comes to social media marketing.

Remember, success in social media marketing comes from interacting and building relationships. Small business owners are typically used to getting directly in front of customers, speaking with them, learning about them, listening to them, and engaging them. Big businesses are often used to managing consumers at arm's length. Furthermore, small businesses can jump into conversations, try new tools, and modify their strategies and tactics on the fly, while big businesses have to go through countless meetings and deep hierarchical battles to get permission to change a single word on their websites, let alone jump onboard with a new social media tool or alter a strategy or tactic. In other words, the social Web moves quickly, giving small businesses an advantage over big businesses that have trouble getting out of their own way.

Additionally, small businesses are more accepting of the lack of hard-number metrics available to track the success of social media marketing. Like brand building, much of your effort at social media marketing will add intangible value to your business's bottom line but will be difficult to track. For big businesses, a lack of tangible metrics can be a big problem. Small business owners are more receptive to the concept of building quality relationships over the need to boost the quantity of relationships, which is a fundamental and undeniable truth of social media marketing. Quality trumps quantity every time on the social Web.

Laura Fitton of Pistachio Consulting and author of *Twitter for Dummies* is a perfect example of an entrepreneur leveraging the tools of the social Web to build a successful business. In 2007, Laura signed up for an account on a new website, http://twitter.com. She quickly realized how powerful Twitter could be, and in September 2008, she revived her business, Pistachio Consulting, with a new focus on teaching clients how to use Twitter and social media to build their own businesses. Laura went from being a stay-at-home mom with two children under the age of two to the owner of a thriving company and a published author, simply because she was able to jump onboard quickly, make mistakes, learn, and grow. Most big businesses didn't even see the value in Twitter until 2009, when Laura's business had already been thriving for well over a year.

Small businesses can also use the tools of the social Web to level the competitive playing field. The Roger Smith Hotel in New York City found its niche in the competitive Manhattan travel market thanks to Twitter. Through its @RSHotel Twitter profile, the Roger Smith Hotel offers special Twitter discounts to followers and actively tries to build relationships through its public Twitter stream and private direct messages without ever directly selling. Over time, word started to spread across the social Web about the small hotel that truly cares about its guests. Staff members make a point of greeting all guests in person who come to the hotel via the social Web, with the goal of building trust with each person and showing each customer that he or she can truly believe in the brand promise the Roger Smith Hotel communicates through the social Web.

The Three Cs of Social Media Marketing Success or Failure

Truth be told, there really is no right or wrong way to participate in the social Web conversation. However, if you want to be a welcomed participant, you should adhere to some basic rights and wrongs. These rights and wrongs are more like acceptable standards of behavior than participation rules. Just as there are unwritten rules of behavior that guide you in your daily life, there are similar rules on the social Web. People have expectations of how others should act on the social Web. That's not to say there aren't people who flout those rules, but it's safe to say that few of those people are very popular on the social Web. There's a fine line between behaving on the social Web in ways that help you build bridges and acting in ways that cause those bridges to collapse (taking your messages along with them).

There are three primary behavioral areas that you need to be aware of and adhere to when you join the social Web if you want your social media marketing efforts to succeed. I call these three behavioral areas the three Cs of social media marketing success or failure, summarized in Table 3.1.

Businesses that allow the online conversation to flow at the hands of consumers are positioned for success, while businesses that try to control the conversation and hold tight reins on it will fail. Of course, there are exceptions to every rule, but for long-term success in social media marketing, the free flow of content across the social Web is essential.

Providing useful information, interacting, and being personable are all critical elements of social media success, but they're not the only elements. You also need to be accessible, which means you need to surround your audience with your brand, so people can pick and

TABLE 3.1 The Three Cs of Social Media Marketing Success or Failure

	WRONG (FAILURE)	RIGHT (SUCCESS)
Conversation	Stop it.	Let it flow.
Content	Copyright-protect it, or put up a barrier to access it.	Share it.
Control	Hold it tightly.	Give it up.

choose where they're comfortable engaging with you. Not all consumers like to read blogs, nor do all consumers like to read Twitter updates. As you learned earlier in this chapter, you need to do some research as you embark on your social Web journey and find out where your target audience spends time. Then you can join the conversation and begin to publish your own branded content.

Chapter 4

Warning: One Size Does Not Fit All

The title of this chapter sums up social media marketing strategy with a six-word warning. By saying one size does not fit all, I mean there is no single recipe for success with social media marketing. Instead, each company has its own unique social media marketing strategy, and so should you. As you venture into the world of social media marketing, you'll be tempted to copy your competitors. By doing so, you'll be marketing scared and from a reactive position rather than from a proactive position. Don't be tempted to follow others, because what other businesses are doing with social media marketing might not be right for your business. That's why there is no single action plan, schedule, or template that a small business owner should follow to implement his or her own social media marketing plan.

As you learned in Chapter 3, you need to be aware of what other businesses (particularly your competitors) are doing on the social Web, because you can certainly learn from them. However, no one is truly an expert in social media marketing, because it's still in its infancy. Large companies, small companies, and every company in between are still in the testing stage when it comes to leveraging the tools of the social Web to build businesses. In fact, if you ask 10 social media marketing professionals to create a social media marketing strategy for your business, you'll probably get 10 different answers. But guess what? That's OK.

Many tools are available for little or no cost to help you market your business through the social Web. These include blogs, Twitter, Facebook, LinkedIn, YouTube, Flickr, and many more. You need to understand your business, audience, and goals before you can determine where to start your efforts at social media marketing. At the same time, you need to understand that using these tools requires a time investment. Not only do you need to select tools and initiatives that fit into your schedule, but you also need to experiment with them and find the tools you actually *like* to use.

Realistically, the majority of people who own small and midsize businesses don't have the money to hire teams of people to actually *do* social media marketing for them on a daily basis, so they have to do it themselves. It stands to reason that if you don't like Twitter, then you won't be motivated to update your Twitter status throughout the day. If your efforts at social media marketing aren't enjoyable for you, then you won't use them enough to be successful, and your passion about your business won't shine through. As a result, you won't make the quality connections and build the relationships you need for building your business. But if you love to create videos, you can start a YouTube channel where you can share your video content. The choice is yours.

Bottom line, you must first experiment with different tools to find the ones you actually enjoy and want to spend more time using. Soon, interacting with your online connections won't seem like work. Instead, it will be fun, and you might just find yourself spending more time on the social Web than you expected and without complaint. Ultimately, your social Web presence will expand into new activities, which effectively surround people with opportunities to build relationships with you.

Take the case of NakedPizza. This company maintains a diverse social media presence. NakedPizza is an excellent company to watch and learn from on the social Web.

NakedPizza opened its doors in New Orleans in 2006. With the costs of direct mail (a medium that pizza restaurants rely on heavily) soaring and response rates plummeting, NakedPizza turned to the social Web for new marketing opportunities. In March 2009, NakedPizza joined Twitter in an effort to save on marketing costs while building relationships that could lead to sales. Before 2009 came to a close, Twitter had become an integral part of NakedPizza's growing business. The company set a new in-store sales record on May 29, 2009, with 68 percent of sales on that day generated by customers who came to NakedPizza by way of Twitter. Throughout 2009, NakedPizza expanded its social Web presence and activity to ultimately include a blog, Facebook page, and Flickr and foursquare profiles, and business was thriving.

Five Steps to Successful Social Media Marketing

Consumers have more choices than ever, thanks to the ease of finding information online, and the social Web has opened up a global online conversation that most companies still don't know how to leverage. That's because companies aren't willing to accept the three keys to social media marketing success:

1. Brand consistency in image and message, which creates a brand promise
2. Setting and meeting customer expectations based on the brand promise
3. Letting the audience take control

Not only is social media marketing an excellent opportunity for building relationships, brand loyalty, and business, but it's also an amazing tool for search engine optimization, opening more doors for people to find you online than anyone could have dreamed of a decade ago. The question today shouldn't be "Why should my business be active on the social Web?" but instead "Why isn't my business already active on the social Web?"

Using the tools of the social Web, you can directly and indirectly promote your business, because every interaction opens a new door to your online presence. That means your social media participation shouldn't be limited to promotional efforts. Instead, you should invite all departments and functions to join your business's social media efforts. Figure 4.1 shows some of the many ways that multiple departments within your business can join the online conversation to build awareness, recognition, and business for you.

Regardless of what department is participating on the social Web or what message is being delivered at any given time, the five basic steps toward success in social media marketing remain constant.

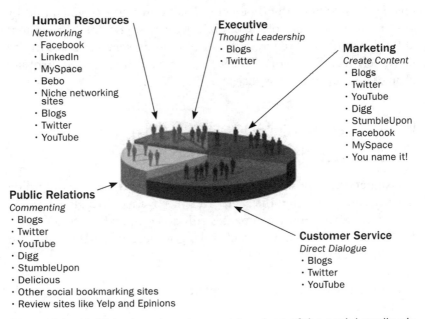

Human Resources
Networking
· Facebook
· LinkedIn
· MySpace
· Bebo
· Niche networking
  sites
· Blogs
· Twitter
· YouTube

Executive
Thought Leadership
· Blogs
· Twitter

Marketing
Create Content
· Blogs
· Twitter
· YouTube
· Digg
· StumbleUpon
· Facebook
· MySpace
· You name it!

Public Relations
Commenting
· Blogs
· Twitter
· YouTube
· Digg
· StumbleUpon
· Delicious
· Other social bookmarking sites
· Review sites like Yelp and Epinions

Customer Service
Direct Dialogue
· Blogs
· Twitter
· YouTube

Figure 4.1   Multiple departments can get a piece of the social media pie.

You'll have to experiment with tools and tactics, as discussed earlier in this chapter, to find the mix that works best for you, your audience, and your business, but the basic steps remain the same with each new initiative you pursue on the social Web.

Step 1: Find Your Best Audience

The Internet is a crowded, cluttered place, and it doesn't matter how great your social media marketing efforts are if you're not spending time in the right places on the social Web. Before you do anything else related to social media marketing, you must invest time in finding the people you want to communicate with online. Once you find them, you can join the conversation where they're already spending time. Eventually, you can work to guide them over to your own blog, Twitter stream, and so on, where they can find more of your amazing content and continue to strengthen their relationships with you.

QUICK TIP

Conduct a Google blog search (http://blogsearch.google.com) or an advanced Twitter search (http://search.twitter.com/advanced) to find people discussing subjects related to your business.

Step 2: Create Great Content

What you *say* on the social Web is the most important element of your social media marketing success or failure. In Chapter 2, you learned about creating amazing content, and that content should be the cornerstone of your online presence. Make sure your tone and writing style are human, honest, and transparent, and most important, make sure your personality shines through. No one wants to build a relationship with a machine or a com-

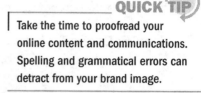

QUICK TIP

Take the time to proofread your online content and communications. Spelling and grammatical errors can detract from your brand image.

pany blowhard, and that's exactly how you'll be perceived if you keep your personality hidden behind jargon and rhetoric.

Step 3: Never Stop Researching

Not only should you keep tabs on what your competitors are doing on the social Web, but you should also know what your target customers are doing. Find out what kind of information they're looking for, what engages them and what keeps them coming back for more, and then give them those things. You should also find businesses and people outside of your industry who are doing great things on the social Web. Benchmark their tactics, identify the ones that are relevant to your business and goals, and apply them to your own social media marketing strategy.

QUICK TIP

Determine the keywords your audience is likely to use in online searches to find a business like yours, using tools like Wordtracker (www.wordtracker.com), Keyword Discovery (www.keyworddiscovery .com), or the Google AdWords keyword tool (https://adwords.google .com/select/KeywordToolExternal). Then sign up to receive e-mail alerts when those keywords are found by Google (www.google.com/alerts) or Twitter (www.tweetbeep.com).

Step 4: Give More than You Receive

As you learned in Chapter 3, you should spend far more time building relationships and communicating *with* people on the social Web than you spend self-promoting or talking *at* people on the social Web. Don't just publicize company news. Instead, give your

QUICK TIP

Set a timer to keep you on track with your social Web efforts each day. It's very easy to get lost in "Internet time," and suddenly hours have passed when you thought you'd only been interacting for minutes.

audience interesting, useful, and valuable content and communications. Answer questions, ask your own, and be accessible. Remember the 80-20 rule discussed in Chapter 3, and try to spend at least 80 percent of your time on the social Web interacting with people and no more than 20 percent self-promoting.

Step 5: Diversify Your Social Web Activities

Don't put all your eggs in one basket. As you become more comfortable on the social Web, test new tools, join conversations on other sites, and spread your online brand further. Doing so allows you to connect with a broader audience and build your network of brand advocates. As your online efforts grow, you need to be certain that you stay active on your various social media profiles. In other words, when you find a new tool you like or get a big response from, don't abandon it. A few minutes spent updating and engaging is better than none if a tool has proven to yield positive results for your business.

> **QUICK TIP**
>
> As you find new tools you enjoy and plan to stick with, be sure to link your social Web profiles together if possible, and promote them on your blog, website, e-mail signature, and so on to increase your connections. For example, add your blog feed to your Facebook and Twitter profiles using a tool like Twitterfeed (http://twitterfeed.com).

Don't Get Overwhelmed, Get Going

The social Web can be intimidating. New tools are popping up every day, and it might seem like it's just too big for a small business to infiltrate. However, the reality of the social Web environment is just the opposite. In 2009, social Web use surpassed e-mail use for the first time, and with smart phones making it easier to update a Twitter profile than it is to make a phone call, the shift from traditional media and forms of communication to new media isn't likely to slow down anytime in the near future.

That's why it's so important that you get involved on the social Web sooner rather than later, or else your business will be left behind. People are online, and they're actively using the social Web to find products, services, businesses, and more. Your business needs to be there. Don't be afraid to start off slowly. Choose a half hour each day to devote to social media marketing activities. Remember, simply responding to comments and sending friend requests counts as actively participating on the social Web.

Choose a time during the day that fits your schedule, and then divide that time between interacting, creating content, reaching out to new connections, and so on. The more you use the tools of the social Web, the easier it becomes. You'll find yourself falling into a comfortable pattern of social media activities. Just don't get complacent. Remember, the social Web is always changing, and you need to continually do your research so you can realign and maximize your efforts in terms of the time you invest and the returns you receive.

Realizing You Need Help

If you simply can't find the time to participate on the social Web or have absolutely no knowledge of how to use a computer or the Internet, your business can still have an active online presence. There are many social media consulting companies that can manage your business's social Web activities for you—strategizing, creating content, communicating, and even analyzing results. But keep in mind that a full-scale social media strategy could cost $5,000 or more. Ongoing consultation and management could run you another $5,000 or more every six months. Separately, creating content each month could cost you thousands of dollars more.

Fortunately, a lot of freelancers are able to help you create content and manage the day-to-day activities of your social Web presence. There are a variety of websites where you can publish job opportunities for bloggers, tweeters, social media writers, and more. Some of these sites are listed in the sidebar "Popular Websites for Finding Freelancers." Freelancers work for themselves and often charge lower rates than full-scale social media marketing companies, simply because their overhead is lower. (Their skills and experience are often just as good as or better than those you'll get from many full-scale companies.)

Before you hire a company, consultant, or freelancer to help you with your social media marketing efforts, you need to make sure they know what they're doing. Many people promote themselves online as social media experts but don't have the true experience or credentials

POPULAR WEBSITES FOR FINDING FREELANCERS

- ProBlogger (www.problogger.net)

- Elance (www.elance.com)

- oDesk (www.odesk.com)

- iFreelance (www.ifreelance.com)

- craigslist (www.craigslist.org)

- BloggingPro (www.bloggingpro.com)

- Freelance Writing Jobs (www.freelancewritinggigs.com)

- Guru (www.guru.com)

- FreelanceSwitch (www.freelanceswitch.com)

to back up their claims. Make sure you view samples of their work, have in-depth discussions about your business and goals with them, and review their social media profiles to be certain they can actually do what they claim they can.

Before you hire a freelancer or company to help you with your social media marketing, you need to define what you want that person or company to do for you. Experienced freelancers and companies will ask you the right questions. For example, if you're hiring a blogger, candidates should ask you how long you want posts to be, if you want images included, if the blogger will be responsible for adding tags and categories, if the blogger will be responsible for managing comments, and more. Each of these tasks affects how long it takes for a blog post to be written and published, and an experienced blogger will want to set expectations and time requirements up front. A single blog post could cost you anywhere from $5 to $100 or more, depending on the experience and abilities of the blogger. As with most things in life, you get what you pay for, so choose wisely when you select someone to help you with your social media marketing.

Experienced professionals should also ask you questions to learn about your business, competitors, audience, brand image and message, goals, and budget. Then they should be able to give you an outline of the types of services they can offer to help you meet your goals.

If they don't ask probing questions in order to truly understand your business and your goals, then a red flag should go up. The person or company that handles your social media marketing should be your *partner*. Being a partner requires fully understanding your business in order to be able to talk about it passionately and build meaningful relationships for you.

Chapter 5

Before You Begin: Perceptions, Honesty, and Giving Up Control

No matter how much money, time, and effort you invest in social media marketing, your efforts are for naught if you don't allow consumers to take control of the online conversation. In fact, it's this fundamental requirement of social media marketing success that most businesses can't accept. If you can't recognize that the power of the social Web and the word-of-mouth marketing it can generate comes from handing over the reins to consumers, then you'll find your goals always stay out of reach.

"But what if someone says something negative or untrue about my business?" you ask.

You're not alone in having that question, but you'll set yourself apart from the crowd if you embrace the fact that there are ways to manage the online buzz about your business without appearing to be controlling it. In Chapter 3, you learned two very important lessons from the social media marketing mistakes of Dell and United Airlines:

1. Don't try to stop the online conversation.
2. You can only ignore the online conversation for so long.

Frankly, giving up control on the social Web fits in perfectly with consumer expectations for businesses and brands in the 21st century. We live in a time when consumers are more cynical than ever. They distrust businesses and actively seek out companies that appear to be honest and transparent in their business dealings and communications. The social Web offers the perfect platform for you to demonstrate your honesty, admit your mistakes (if you make them), and show people that you care about them and want to make things right.

For example, in 2010, Toyota came under scrutiny after a series of vehicle recalls in the United States. Negative publicity against Toyota was everywhere, including on the social Web. However, Toyota embraced the social Web as a medium that offered the company a place to share its side of the story, to keep consumers up to date with how the company was trying to remedy its mistakes, and to engage Toyota brand loyalists who advocated and protected the brand against negative attacks.

The early months of 2010 were not happy times for Toyota, but the social Web gave the company an outlet where it could try to present both sides of a very unpleasant story. Toyota viewed social media as a tool to distribute relevant information. Rather than attacking the company's detractors, Toyota allowed consumers to provide their views. In other words, instead of attempting to create two separate and distinct sides to the Toyota recall topic, the company used social media as a tool to answer questions and appear accessible and transparent after the company had so clearly failed.

The bottom line is that your social media marketing efforts depend on your ability to listen, add value, and be honest. Unless you exercise those three abilities, your online brand will be meaningless and forgotten. You have to ensure that your audience's perception of your business and brand measures up to these standards at all times. Otherwise, your audience will be confused or feel betrayed. People will turn away from your brand, and you'll learn that while good news can travel across the social Web quickly, bad news can travel 10 times faster.

The 2008 U.S. presidential election campaign offers another excellent example of using the social Web to present an honest and open brand image. Then-Senator Barack Obama and his campaign team became actively involved with social media, particularly on Twitter, in an effort to present a promise of transparency. Obama capitalized on a message of inclusion and change that mirrored the open communication platform that social media provides. It was a good fit and certainly helped him to connect with the online community and create the perception that he walked the walk of which he spoke. It's

TRUE STORY

When Jonathan Schwartz, CEO of Sun Microsystems, wanted to publicly announce his resignation, he did so in the form of a haiku, which he published on his Twitter stream.

safe to assume that no presidential election campaign in the future will happen without a strong social Web presence from all candidates.

After President Obama took office in 2009, his team continued to demonstrate an understanding of the social Web's reach and power. They began publishing weekly presidential address videos on YouTube and stayed active on Twitter. Obama's presidency marked a turning point in how government communicates with the people.

What to Do When Things Get Ugly

No matter how hard you try, someone is going to say something negative about your business on the social Web at some time. When that inevitable day arrives, you have three main choices that you can make in reaction, which I refer to as flight, fight, or flood.

Flight: Ignore It

The easiest course of action is to ignore negative information about you online. This strategy is actually very effective when the negativity is from a single or small source and doesn't travel far. The "squeaky wheel" will move on to attack something else, and your lack of response will allow the negative comments to fade away into the oblivion of the Internet. But don't forget the story of United Airlines told in Chapter 3. You must stay on top of the online conversation, so you know when it's time to step in and respond.

Fight: Respond to It

If negative information about your company finds its way online, you may want to respond to it. While you certainly should not use a heavy-handed, defensive tone in your response, you should work to massage perceptions and nudge the conversation in the right direction. If you're accessible, willing to help fix problems, and truly interested in the people you come in contact with on the social Web, then a negative conversation can be addressed and, ultimately, turn into a positive interaction that paints you in an even better light.

Just be careful not to be tempted into heated debates or attacks. Some people spend time online for the sole purpose of riling up others. The more time you spend online, the more easily you will recognize the pot stirrers. Always consider the source before you respond, and then act accordingly.

Flood: Bury It

The majority of people find information and businesses through a search on their preferred search engines, such as Google. When people conduct a keyword search for which the results should include links to your business website, you certainly don't want the results to be filled with links that offer negative information about you. This is where your amazing content becomes important again. The more great content you publish that people share, link to, and discuss online, the better chance you have of flooding the Web with positive content and getting the results you want to appear high in searches for your business-related keywords, rather than the negative results you want to bury.

Search Engine Reputation Management Matters

Each of the choices listed in the preceding section is part of a practice known as search engine reputation management (SERM), which involves monitoring your chosen keywords as well as your brand name, business name, and so on, to ensure that the results returned in search engine queries are the ones you want to be returned. Many companies and consultants work exclusively with businesses to ensure their SERM is the best it can be. SEOmoz (www.seomoz.org) has an excellent website and online community for learning more about SERM from experts and practitioners. Most importantly, you need to monitor your name and keyword search results (as discussed in Chapter 4), create amazing content that helps build your reputation and incoming links, develop online relationships with other people who will share and link to your content, and write content with search engine optimization techniques in mind (see "SERM Quick Tips").

SERM QUICK TIPS

1. Get your brand name in your domain name, Twitter ID, Facebook profile, Facebook page, YouTube channel, and so on before someone else uses it.
2. Monitor your brand mentions online.
3. Flood the Web with your amazing content to ensure your intended brand messages appear highest in Google search results and bury negativity.
4. Invest in legitimate SEO help through sites like SEOmoz.org or a consultant specializing in search engine optimization if you need it.

The Power of the Online Community

The online community can drive change—both for the better and for the worse. The collective voices of Internet users can get loud and spread far and wide. That's a story that the Wisconsin Tourism Federation learned in July 2009, when a new name and logo caused a stir across the social Web. The primary component of the organization's logo was an acronym: WTF. In the United States, *WTF?* also represents a fairly obscene yet common expletive. When the story of the Wisconsin Tourism Federation's error started spreading across the social Web, the organization decided that the right course of action was to respond. Despite investing a lot of money into the new name and logo design, by October 2009, the Wisconsin Tourism Federation changed its name to the Tourism Federation of Wisconsin, and the logo's acronym became TFW. An embarrassing story made its way across the social Web, and a response was the best course of action.

As your online network of connections grows and your relationships with them develop, they'll become loyal brand advocates and guardians. When negative information appears online about you or your business, your network of brand advocates and guardians are likely to come to your rescue, speak up in your defense, and help you bury negative or erroneous content. Your online network is extremely powerful. That's why it is absolutely essential that you spend the majority of your time on the social Web building relationships, not self-promoting. And that's why it's so important that you present yourself as human and honest, rather than controlling and manipulative. Let the online conversation flow for maximum results. For another

HARRY POTTER'S RISE FROM CHILDREN'S FANTASY BOOK TO A GLOBAL PHENOMENON

When J. K. Rowling's first book in the Harry Potter series was released in England in 1997, no one imagined that the story of a boy wizard could grow into the global phenomenon that it is today. However, Harry Potter didn't become a worldwide sensation overnight, nor did Harry Potter become a worldwide sensation as the result of a big marketing budget. In reality, Harry Potter became a multibillion-dollar brand at the hands of consumers who talked about it and made it their own, particularly on the social Web.

Early in the Harry Potter life cycle, Rowling and her publishers agreed that trying to stop the online conversation was a mistake. While their first reaction to fan sites and blogs was to send cease-and-desist letters, they quickly realized that the power of the online conversation could do far more good than harm. Consumers took control of the brand, shared it, and personalized it. They created a wide variety of online brand experiences, including fan fiction and music, fan art, and forums. Not a stone was left unturned in terms of how consumers interacted with and personalized their experiences of the Harry Potter brand. By 2000, when the fourth book in the Harry Potter series was released, the boy wizard was a household name around the world, and it all came as the result of word-of-mouth marketing and an online buzz from consumers who were given the opportunity to live the brand they love.

example of how powerful the social Web community can be, see the story "Harry Potter's Rise from Children's Fantasy Book to a Global Phenomenon."

The Next Steps for Social Media Marketing Success

Never before in history have businesses had access to so many people as today, thanks to the social Web. You can get real-time feedback and direct dialogue with consumers, build trust, and develop relationships that transcend a single transaction. Furthermore, the social Web is a medium where business-to-consumer, business-to-business, *and* consumer-to-consumer conversations can flourish. Don't look at social media marketing as a burden. Instead, look at it as an opportunity to learn and grow. Some of the relationships you develop through your social media efforts could grow into more than you ever imagined. Many entrepreneurs have found their small businesses grow into global companies, thanks to the power of the social Web. Remember the story of Gary Vaynerchuk told in Chapter 2. In simplest terms, the social Web is what you make of it.

With that in mind, you should make some commitments before you dive into the social Web conversation. If you can't commit to your social media marketing plan, particularly these three specific commitments, then don't even bother:

- I will dedicate at least 30 minutes each day to social media activities.
- I will invest in social media marketing for the long term because I understand that success requires patience and persistence.
- I will allow myself to have fun.

If you're ready to commit to leveraging the social Web to build your business, then you're on your way to continual learning, fun, and success. In Part II of this book, you can learn how to use a variety of social Web tools for direct and indirect marketing, but before you continue, you need to consider your ultimate goals for your social media marketing efforts and understand how they correlate with the 10 basic steps of social media marketing (see "Social Media Marketing in 10 Steps"). These steps outline the various concepts and theories discussed throughout Part I. Read them, understand them, apply them to your social media marketing goals, and keep them in mind throughout your journey on the social Web. If you stick to these steps, your efforts at social media marketing can't fail.

SOCIAL MEDIA MARKETING IN 10 STEPS

1. Identify your ultimate goals.
2. Determine the brand image, message, and promise you want to portray on the social Web.
3. Find your best audience (or audiences).
4. Create messages and content that consistently communicate your brand promise to draw your audience to your online destination.
5. Diversify your social media presence to broaden your audience and network.
6. Join the online conversation across the social Web, and build your network of brand advocates.
7. Allow the online community to take control of the conversation.
8. Be real, be honest, be accessible, be engaging, and be true to your brand promise.
9. Test, analyze results, and try again.
10. Be consistent and persistent, and don't give up.

PART II

Test the Water

The Where of Social Media Marketing

Chapter 6

Analyzing Social Media Marketing Tools

When you start your journey into social media marketing, the first thing you'll realize is that there are a lot of ways to join the online conversation. The number and variety of tools and opportunities can be completely overwhelming. Where do you begin? The first step is to identify the different kinds of social Web tools that you can use for social media marketing.

You can participate on the social Web in four primary ways, which I call the four Cs of social media marketing participation: content creation, content sharing, connections, and community building. Multiple tools are available to help you participate in all of the four Cs. In fact, some tools of the social Web allow you to participate in the online conversation in more ways than one. Table 6.1 shows a handful of social media marketing tools you can use, making it clear that there are a lot of choices. Remember, some of the tools listed in Table 6.1 can actually fit into more than one category. For example, Ning is both a community-building tool and a social networking tool. You can find even more tools in Appendix B.

QUICK TIP

This book introduces many of the most popular tools of social media marketing, but many other tools available online can be used for social media marketing. Some less-popular tools reach broad audiences, and others reach highly focused, niche audiences. Don't be afraid to test tools that are not discussed in this book if they appear to reach your target audience.

TABLE 6.1 Popular Social Media Marketing Tools

CONTENT CREATION	CONTENT SHARING	CONNECTIONS	COMMUNITY BUILDING
WordPress	Twitter	Facebook	Ning
Blogger	Plurk	LinkedIn	Google Groups
TypePad	Jaiku	Google Buzz	Facebook pages
Movable Type	Tumblr	MySpace	Facebook
LiveJournal	Digg	Bebo	groups
YouTube	Reddit	Xanga	LinkedIn groups
Dailymotion	StumbleUpon	foursquare	Forums
blip.tv	Yahoo! Buzz	Jaiku	
Viddler	Delicious	Orkut	
Vimeo	Propeller		
TubeMogul.com	Newsvine		
Blubrry	Fark		
iTunes	Slashdot		
BlogTalkRadio	SlideShare		
Flickr			
Picasa			
E-books			
Online seminars			
Virtual conferences			
Associated Content			
EzineArticles.com			
Squidoo			
Epinions			
Yelp			
CitySearch			
City Guides			

As you learned in Part I, it's important to test different tools to determine which you enjoy using and which provide an opportunity for you to interact with your target audience. Ultimately, you want to participate in all four methods of social media marketing to ensure your messages reach the widest audience. In Part II, you will learn about some of the most popular tools of the social Web, so you have a starting point for your own social media marketing initiatives. You can then build your social media marketing plan, strategy, and tactics as you experiment, network, and learn.

Content Creation as Social Media Marketing

The cornerstone of any social media marketing strategy is creating amazing content. Before you can reach out to other people on the social Web and build relationships with them, you need to prove you have something interesting or valuable to say, and you have to demonstrate that you can be trusted. You can do that by creating an ongoing repository of content that positions you as an authoritative, contributing member of the social Web community.

But what kind of content should you create? The truth of the matter is that there is no specific type of content that you must publish to be a welcome member of the social Web community. On the contrary, your content should uniquely represent your personality and business, and a variety of tools can help you create that content. For example, you can start a blog and publish informative posts. You can create a YouTube channel and upload interviews with customers or video tutorials. You can even start a Twitter profile and share interesting articles and information you find online as well as tips and tidbits about you and your business. Throw in the occasional exclusive offer for your online followers, and you're on your way to developing a strong social Web presence with amazing content.

Creating content not only helps you establish credibility, but also can help consumers, build relationships and loyalty, and boost your efforts at search engine optimization. The more great content you publish, the better. Think of the story about Gary Vaynerchuk told in Chapter 2. Gary's *Wine Library* store grew to a business generating $50 million per year, thanks to the amazing content he published on the social Web in the form of blog posts, videos, Twitter updates, and more. You can do it, too!

SOCIAL MEDIA MARKETING PARTICIPATION METHOD 1

First, start creating content now. You can write a blog, post updates on Twitter, create online videos, produce podcasts, publish photos, write online articles, write e-books, host webinars, hold virtual conferences, share online tutorials, and more!

Content Sharing as Social Media Marketing

Just as you need to create great content to prove your worth on the social Web, you also need to acknowledge and help other members of the social Web community by sharing their content with your audience. The classic proverb "Give and you shall receive" definitely applies on the social Web. Giving other people a pat on the back and showing that you appreciate their content and effort enough to share it with your own audience are critical parts of building relationships on the social Web, particularly with online influencers. It's important to get on the radar screen of online influencers, and when you share their content, you have a good chance of being noticed and remembered. In the future, they might share your content.

When other people reciprocate and share your content with their connections, your content gets in front of a much larger audience. Some of those people might connect with you directly or share your content further, thereby broadening your online audience even more. Sharing content can lead to indirect and direct sales, depending on the type of content being shared. For example, coupon codes listed on Twitter can be shared and redeemed, just as useful blog posts about your industry can be shared. The former can lead to direct sales, while the latter can generate an increase in brand awareness, brand recognition, and brand loyalty, which can lead to indirect sales.

SOCIAL MEDIA MARKETING PARTICIPATION METHOD 2

Start sharing content. You can share links to interesting and helpful articles, blog posts, pictures, videos, and so on with Twitter, Facebook, LinkedIn, Digg, StumbleUpon, Tumblr, and more.

Connecting as Social Media Marketing

It's hard to believe that not too long ago, people could network only at face-to-face meetings, conferences, and events. Today, you can network with people around the world for personal and professional reasons from the comfort of your own home. It's convenient, educational, and fun. Social networking lets you meet more people who share similar interests with you than you can imagine, and with that networking, you can build relationships that can lead to more business.

The rules of networking in person apply to social networking, too. The most important thing to remember is that your words live online for a long time. Use caution and restraint in your communications while staying human and honest. If you can strike that balance, you're on the right track to social networking success. Also, make sure that your social networking profiles are open for the public to see. If necessary, create separate social networking profiles for your business and personal connections, but keep your business profiles accessible to everyone. A private profile can't help you get in front of a larger audience via the social Web.

SOCIAL MEDIA MARKETING PARTICIPATION METHOD 3

Create complete profiles on social networking sites like Facebook and LinkedIn, and then find people you know and start sending connection requests to them. Also, spend time updating your profile status and sharing content. Link your blog and Twitter feeds to your social networking profiles, so your status updates automatically with links to your latest content.

Community Building as Social Media Marketing

The social Web is one big online community of individuals who enjoy interacting with people across the globe using technology. Hundreds of millions of people spend time on the social Web each day, and each person has different reasons for being there. The trick for businesses is finding niche communities interested in their products and services, and then connecting with them and building relationships with them.

You can either find an existing community that matches your business or build your own online community to support your business. Many social networking sites provide features that allow you to join and create online communities. Using the Groups feature in Facebook or LinkedIn, you can find a huge variety of groups to join, or within minutes, you can create your own group and invite people to join, share content, and start conversations. Google Groups also boasts a large variety of existing groups. Additionally, there are also tools that allow you to create your own social network, which enables you to build your own branded community from the ground up. Ning (www.ning.com) is a popular service for creating your own social network, although there is a fee attached to using it.

Online forums are another excellent way to find built-in online communities. Alternately, there are applications that allow you to start your own forum that can be linked to your website or blog.

The advantage of online communities in terms of marketing your business is the inherent interest a community of like-minded people can bring to you. For example, an organic foods store could start an online forum where people can discuss organic foods, ingredients, new products, health, and more. Similarly, that organic foods store could join an existing Facebook group related to healthy living. Both initiatives offer opportunities to connect with audiences likely to be interested in the products the store sells. If the business owner works to make sure participation in the forum and group adds value, then more people will become aware of the brand. The ultimate goal is reached when that awareness turns into word-of-mouth marketing through content sharing and into indirect business through brand loyalty and advocacy.

SOCIAL MEDIA MARKETING PARTICIPATION METHOD 4

Search Facebook and LinkedIn for existing groups and pages related to your business where your target audience might already spend time, and join relevant groups. Next, begin interacting with people in those groups and sharing content. You can do the same thing with Google Groups, Ning, and forums.

15 Ways to Jump-Start Your Social Media Marketing Plan

In Part I, you learned that there really is no right or wrong way to do social media marketing. That's an important point to bear in mind as you review the sample plans and suggestions for developing your own social media marketing strategy in this book and elsewhere. Only you can determine the best social media marketing strategy for your business based on your budget, time, technical ability, and interests. With that in mind, don't be afraid to test new tools, but also don't be afraid to forgo using a tool you don't enjoy. Try to be patient and give each new tool its fair chance, but don't try to force yourself each day to use a tool you dread. Your disdain will show through and harm your results rather than help your efforts.

You're probably still feeling overwhelmed, and that's fine. Take a deep breath and just dive in. The social Web does get less intimidating the more you participate in it. While there is always something new to learn, your apprehension will fade as you engage more with other people. Following are 15 suggestions to help you dive into the world of social media marketing, with at least one link for each to a website where you can get started:

1. Start a business blog: http://wordpress.org
2. Start commenting on blogs related to your business: http://blog search.google.com/?hl=en&tab=wb
3. Start a Twitter profile: http://twitter.com
4. Start a Facebook profile: www.facebook.com
5. Start a Facebook page: http://www.facebook.com/pages/create.php
6. Start a Facebook group: http://www.facebook.com/help/?faq=13034
7. Start a LinkedIn profile: www.linkedin.com
8. Start a LinkedIn group: http://learn.linkedin.com/groups
9. Start a YouTube channel: http://www.youtube.com/create_account?next=%2Fchannels
10. Start a Flickr profile: www.flickr.com
11. Start a podcast or online talk show with BlogTalkRadio: www.blogtalkradio.com
12. Start accounts on social bookmarking sites and share content: http://digg.com or www.stumbleupon.com
13. Start publishing articles online: http://ezinearticles.com or www.goarticles.com
14. Start to use automated widgets to share and promote your content and profiles: http://www.facebook.com/facebook

-widgets/?ref=pf and http://twitter.com/goodies/widgets and http://www.linkedin.com/static?key=developers_widgets&trk =hb_ft_widgets

15. Start getting reviews of your business online: www.yelp.com or www.kudzu.com

These tactics and much more are discussed in detail throughout Parts II and III of this book. While a book that covers all social media marketing opportunities would be too heavy to pick up (and would be out-of-date within a few months as less popular tools meet their demise and new tools are launched), this book introduces you to the tools that should definitely be considered part of your online market-ing arsenal. They're popular, and for the most part, they're free. If for no other reason than boosting your business website's search engine rankings, you should be present on the social Web. Every minute you wait is a missed opportunity.

Chapter 7

Blogging

I t's hard to believe that it wasn't long ago when blogs were simply online diaries, completely disregarded by businesses. Today, the reality is exactly the opposite. Blogs are a critical component of any business's online marketing strategy. If for no other reason, you should publish a business blog to boost the number of people who find your website through search engines.

As you learned in Part I, the vast majority of people search for information about businesses, brands, products, and services online. Your business needs to be represented. When you publish a business blog, each new post you publish creates a new entry point for search engines to index and consumers to find. Furthermore, when you publish amazing blog content, other bloggers and social Web participants might link to your posts to share with their own audiences, and that can lead to even more exposure for your business. No matter what line of business you're in, a business blog can help your business grow.

What Is a Blog, and Why Does Your Business Need One?

A blog is simply a type of website that is created using a blogging application such as WordPress, Blogger, TypePad, or Movable Type and is frequently updated with new articles (called *posts*). Posts are displayed in reverse chronological order with all previous content stored in archives that can be accessed at any time. Blog visitors can join the conversation by submitting comments on posts that interest them. Comments are what make blogs social and help bloggers build relationships with people around the world.

Your business can benefit from having a blog for a variety of reasons:

- **Brand building:** A business blog is a great place to communicate your brand message and promise. By creating content that accurately reflects your brand, you can raise brand awareness, recognition, and loyalty.
- **Marketing tool:** The online buzz is powerful, and a business blog that features useful, interesting, and helpful content can boost the word-of-mouth marketing about your business across the social Web. That conversation can also spread offline.
- **Sales tool:** You can promote products and services directly and indirectly on your business blog and add to your business's bottom line. You can also use your blog as a tool to attract traffic and then drive that traffic to your online catalog or store to encourage direct sales.
- **Customer service:** Blogging is interactive and provides a forum for a two-way conversation with customers. You can use your business blog to share information, answer questions, acquire feedback, and more. Not only does this allow you to build relationships with consumers, but it also can reduce your customer service costs.
- **Relationship building:** When you provide useful information and communicate with consumers on your business blog, their emotional connection to your business grows. Consumers are far more apt to become loyal to you and speak about you to others when they have a relationship with you.
- **Search engine optimization (SEO):** As mentioned at the beginning of this chapter, blogs can deliver a sizable SEO boost.

Large and small businesses can benefit from a business blog. Even entrepreneurs and work-at-home parents have developed successful businesses with the exposure and relationships that business blogs offer. An example is Brian Clark of Copyblogger. Clark started his blog in 2006 as an extension of his online business and writing career. In less than two years, he had developed one of the most successful blogs online, and his career took him in new directions as a social Web celebrity.

You never know what can happen at the hands of the social Web community, but you'll never find out if you don't join the conversation and mark your own online destination. A business blog is the perfect place to make your social Web home base, because you can create a lot of high-quality content on a blog.

It's All About the Content

The success of your business blog depends on the content you publish. If your blog posts aren't interesting, helpful, or useful, then no one is going to want to read them or share them. Think of it this way: if you spend time conversing with someone at a party and have a great conversation, but then you invite that person to your house and the conversation is boring, it's likely that person won't want to come to your house again. The same concept holds true for your business blog. No matter how much fun you are to hang out with on other blogs, in forums, and so on, no one is going to want to come to your blog and hang out if the conversation fizzles there. Your goal is to publish blog posts that get people talking and intrigues them enough to make them want to come back.

Southwest Airlines is very good at creating blog content that keeps people coming back for more. The Southwest Airlines blog, *Nuts about Southwest*, is written by employees who are given the freedom to write in their own voices and share their own stories. A lot of the content on the Southwest Airlines blog is unofficial, highly conversational, and entertaining. Employees and visitors are allowed to take control of the online conversation, allowing them to develop true relationships devoid of corporate rhetoric. That's exactly what you want to do with your business blog.

Naturally, your line of business and target audience will affect the content and language you use to write your blog posts. What remains constant is the need to be human, accessible, and honest. Take a look at "20 Easy Business Blog Post Ideas" for a list of ideas to help you begin writing content on your own business blog.

20 EASY BUSINESS BLOG POST IDEAS

1. Exclusive promotions and discounts
2. Product tutorials
3. Customer interviews
4. Employee interviews
5. Behind-the-scenes look at your company
6. Supplier interviews
7. Industry news
8. Responses to customer questions
9. Highlights of products (e.g., "Secret Uses for . . .")
10. Questions and polls for market research
11. Predictions of trends
12. Demonstrations of how to use a product
13. Reviews of something
14. Lists (e.g., "10 Do's and Don'ts for . . .")
15. Discussion of industry events
16. Photos of your employees, office, etc.
17. Video interviews, demonstrations, etc.
18. Personal insight or opinions
19. Thank-yous
20. Guest blog posts by people you invite to submit articles

Blogging Tools for Businesses

A wide variety of blogging tools are available to help you create a business blog. In fact, you can use a blogging application to create your entire business website! Since blogs are so search-engine-friendly, it's worthwhile to look into using a blog as your central online destination. Don't believe me? Check out the site shown in Figure 7.1, which looks like a website but was actually built using the highly popular Word-Press application available from WordPress.org.

Each blogging application offers similar features, but for business websites and blogs, I recommend the self-hosted version of Word-Press available from WordPress.org, because it's the most flexible. In simplest terms, the self-hosted version of WordPress is free for anyone to use, but you must secure a Web host yourself, which offers the

Figure 7.1　A website built with WordPress

space to store your blog and content as well as the capability to display (or "serve") that content to Web visitors.

Therefore, the self-hosted WordPress application also requires either a bit of technical knowledge to set up or the help of a blog designer or developer to help you get your blog to look and function the way you want it to. Fortunately, you can hire a blog designer to create and customize a blog for you for as little as a few hundred dollars. Actually using a blogging application to publish blog posts is easy if you know how to use the Internet and are familiar with common word processing software. That's because popular blogging applications use simple drag-and-drop features, point-and-click menus, and WYSIWYG (what you see is what you get) editors to make it easy to create and publish content online. Some of the pros and cons of the most popular blogging applications are included in Table 7.1.

If you decide to use the self-hosted WordPress application from WordPress.org and need help designing and setting up your business

> **QUICK TIP**
>
> Check Appendix B for resources that will help you learn how to use various blogging applications and for tools to enhance your business blog.

TABLE 7.1 Popular Blogging Applications

	WORDPRESS .ORG (SELF-HOSTED) (www.wordpress .org)	WORDPRESS .COM/ WORDPRESS-HOSTED/ (www.wordpress .com)	BLOGGER (www.blog ger.com)	TYPEPAD (www.type pad.com)
Ease of use	Easy once the blog is set up. Setup and adding new features may require the help of a blog designer or developer.	Easy	Easy	Easy
Functionality	Advanced	Limited	Moderate	Moderate
Cost	Free, but you have to pay a Web host to store and display your content.	Free with limited functionality. Additional functionality is available at additional costs.	Free	Monthly fee
Domain name	You pay for your own.	Free with .word press.com extension, or you can pay for your own.	Free with .blogspot .com extension, or you can pay for your own.	Free with .typepad .com extension, or you can pay for your own.

blog, a variety of websites will help you find capable people to help you at reasonable prices. Following is a brief list of websites where freelance blog designers and developers look for new clients and projects:

- Elance (www.elance.com)
- oDesk (www.odesk.com)

- Freelancer (www.freelancer.com)
- iFreelance (www.ifreelance.com)
- FreelanceSwitch (www.freelanceswitch.com)
- Guru (www.guru.com)
- craigslist (www.craigslist.org)

WordPress.org offers an open-source WordPress application, meaning the code used to write the application is available to anyone, so developers can create add-on tools that increase the functionality of the application. These tools are called WordPress plugins. The majority are available for free and can enhance your blog and website immensely. For a directory of WordPress plugins to download, go to http://wordpress.org/extend/plugins.

QUICK TIP

To get an idea of how easy it is to use a blogging application, create a free blog at http://wordpress.com or www.blogger.com, and experiment with it. Once you feel comfortable with your test blog, you can create your business blog.

The large number of WordPress plugins can be daunting to bloggers. Don't be afraid to test plugins. You can always deactivate them once you install them. Following are several of the most useful WordPress plugins for business blogs:

- **All-in-One SEO Pack:** Use this plugin to make your blog posts even more search-engine-friendly. http://wordpress.org/extend/plugins/all-in-one-seo-pack
- **Share This:** Use this plugin to make it easy for visitors to share your blog posts on Twitter and popular social networking and bookmarking sites. http://wordpress.org/extend/plugins/share-this
- **Contact Form 7:** Use this plugin to create a contact form for your blog. http://wordpress.org/extend/plugins/contact-form-7
- **Google XML Sitemaps Generator:** Use this plugin to create a sitemap (a hierarchical list of links to all posts and pages on your blog) for your blog. It's great for search engine optimization. http://wordpress.org/extend/plugins/google-sitemap-generator
- **WordPress Database Backup:** Use this plugin to back up your WordPress database, so your data are safe if your Web host experiences a data disaster. http://wordpress.org/extend/plugins/wp-db-backup

Business Blogging Quick-Start Plan Using the WordPress Application

Once you choose the blogging application you want to use to create your business blog, you're ready to get started. But where do you start? The following quick-start plan shows you the main steps to developing your online presence via a business blog using the self-hosted version of WordPress from WordPress.org. With the help of a book like *WordPress for Dummies* by Lisa Sabin-Wilson (Wiley, 2009) or my book *The Complete Idiot's Guide to WordPress* (Alpha/Penguin, 2011), a blog designer, or your own adventurous sense of trial and error (you really can't break anything), you can work through these steps:

1. **Choose a Web host** to store and serve your blog. Popular options can be found in the sidebar "Popular Web Hosts."

 POPULAR WEB HOSTS

There are many Web hosts you can use to host your business blog. For novices, the most important thing to look for is a Web host that offers tools called cPanel and either Fantastico or SimpleScripts, which make it extremely easy to install the WordPress application and create your blog. The following Web hosts are popular among bloggers:

■ BlueHost (www.bluehost.com)

■ Go Daddy (www.godaddy.com)

■ HostGator (www.hostgator.com)

■ HostMonster (www.hostmonster.com)

■ DreamHost (www.dreamhost.com)

■ Just Host (www.justhost.com)

2. **Purchase a domain name** from your Web host or a separate domain name registrar (although your Web host will probably offer special pricing if you purchase your domain name from the host). The most common extensions used for U.S. businesses are .com, .net, and .biz, and .org is used for nonprofit organizations. For domain name ideas, see the sidebar "Five Tips for Choosing a Domain Name."

FIVE TIPS FOR CHOOSING A DOMAIN NAME

You might have your heart set on using a specific domain name for your business blog, but that domain name might not be available. You can easily search for domain name availability on most Web host sites, including the most popular sites. Following are five tips to help you choose an effective domain name:

1. Try to use your business or brand name.
2. You can use keywords related to your business in your domain name.
3. If the domain name you want isn't available, consider using a less popular extension than .com.
4. If the domain name you want isn't available, consider adding additional words or letters.
5. You can make up a word, but remember, misspelling words intentionally or making up unusual words can cause confusion and takes time to build awareness. You don't want to risk losing visitors due to a cumbersome domain name. Numbers and punctuation also can be confusing.

3. **Upload the WordPress application** to your Web host account (or install it using Fantastico or SimpleScripts from your hosting account), and associate it with your domain name. This process varies by Web host, but it's simple, and your Web host should offer instructions and help.

4. **Upload the theme** you want to use, and make changes to customize the appearance of your blog. Free, premium, and custom themes are available from a variety of sources online. Some popular sources are listed in Appendix B. This is the area where you might need help from a blog designer or developer, depending on your technical knowledge.

5. **Configure your blog's settings** related to comments, functionality, and so on to meet your requirements.

6. **Create your content.**

These six steps might appear to oversimplify the process of creating a blog, but it really is that easy. Remember, if you're technically challenged, you can hire a designer or developer to help you.

Blogging Do's and Don'ts

Once you get your business blog set up, you can start publishing content, but before you dive into the blogosphere, you need to understand the laws and unwritten rules of blogging. While there are a few legal requirements bloggers need to be aware of, the majority of the do's and don'ts of blogging are guidelines of acceptable behavior. Just as there are behavioral guidelines that people follow offline as accepted members of society, so are there guidelines for social Web behavior. Follow the suggestions in this section, and you should be a welcomed member of the online community.

Attribute Your Sources

One of the most important parts of success in social media marketing is building relationships, and one of the best ways to do that is by attributing your sources. Doing so not only sends traffic their way, but it's also the right thing to do. You wouldn't write a term paper without attributing your sources! Don't write a blog post without giving credit where credit is due. Often, this can be done with a simple link within your post to the originating source.

Obtain Appropriate Permissions

Don't use customer or client names in your blog posts without obtaining permission first. Also, make sure that any photographs, images, charts, and so on that you include on your blog do not violate copyright laws. In other words, make sure the images you use on your blog are offered with appropriate Creative Commons licenses, or royalty-free copyrights, or make sure you have permission to use them if you're not sure what kind of copyright it holds (sometimes permission might require payment). To learn more about these requirements, see "Copyrights, Creative Commons, and Image Sources."

Don't Discuss Private Information

The words you publish online can spread, and they can live online for a long, long time. Be very careful that you don't publish private company information or personal information about your employees, customers, competitors, or business partners without their permission.

Don't Attack or Air Grievances

Many people take advantage of the anonymity that the Web provides by inciting arguments and publishing offensive information under the

COPYRIGHTS, CREATIVE COMMONS, AND IMAGE SOURCES

Every published item is copyright-protected by the original publisher, including text, images, photos, and so on. It's illegal to republish another person's work without that person's permission. Although there is a gray area of the law called *fair use*, which offers some exceptions to copyright law, the safest course to follow is to republish another person's work only if you have the owner's permission to do so or the work has a copyright license attached to it that allows you to reuse it without payment or permission.

Creative Commons licenses (www.creativecommons.org) were created as a way to provide looser copyright restrictions on published works. For example, if an image you want to use on your blog has a Creative Commons Attribution Commercial license attached to it, you can republish the image on your business blog as long as you attribute the original source. You will learn more about specific types of Creative Commons licenses in Chapter 10.

A variety of websites post images that are safe to use on your blog. Here are some examples:

- morgueFile (www.morguefile.com)

- stock.xchng (www.sxc.hu)

- PicApp (www.picapp.com)

- Dreamstime (www.dreamstime.com)

- FreeFoto.com (www.freefoto.com)

guise of that anonymity. While it can be tempting to attack back, don't do it. Furthermore, leave your problems offline. You should try to let your personality shine through, but always retain a professional image befitting of your business's brand promise.

Don't Ignore Your Readers

One of the biggest mistakes you can make on the social Web is ignoring your readers. Remember, the biggest benefit of the social Web is building relationships, so you must make an effort to engage your readers and respond to them in a timely manner that not only acknowledges them but makes them feel like valued members of your online community.

Hiring a Business Blogger

If writing doesn't come easily to you or you can't find the time to write new content for your business blog each week, then you can enlist an employee to blog for you. Alternately, you can hire a professional blogger to help you. Keep in mind that professional bloggers come in all shapes and sizes, meaning the level of skills and experiences they bring to the table runs the gamut. The most important thing you want from a blogger is a person who understands how to use the tools of the social Web and can write content your audience will want to read.

A good blogger should be able to show you examples of his or her work, and that work should be well written and free from grammatical and spelling errors. Experienced bloggers can write content for a wide variety of subjects with search engine optimization in mind. While they're likely to have areas of expertise, a professional writer who knows his or her way around the social Web can adjust writing styles to match your requirements and research topics accordingly to create compelling content for your blog. Don't be afraid to ask a potential blogger to write a sample post for you after you have described what you're looking for, so you can determine if the writer can create the kind of content you want.

Before you search for a blogger, you should create a set of guidelines for the blogger to follow to ensure that he or she understands any rules you might have. Sample blog and social media participation guidelines can be found in Chapter 20. You also need to put together a list of expectations and responsibilities for that blogger. Your list should include these requirements:

- How often you want the blog updated
- How long posts should be
- Whether you'll provide the blogger with post topics or the blogger will need to come up with topics to write about
- Whether the blogger needs to find acceptable images, videos, and so on to include with posts
- Any requirements for the blogger to moderate and respond to comments
- Any requirements for the blogger to promote the blog and drive traffic to it
- The tone and voice the blogger should use when writing

- Whether the blogger is expected to include links, tags, and categories in blog posts
- Whether the blogger needs to use or maintain special features in your blog, such as WordPress plugins that require additional time

Just as bloggers come with a wide range of skills and experience, they can also be hired for a wide range of pay rates. Typically, business bloggers are paid an hourly rate, a rate per post, or a monthly fee for a set amount of work. For example, beginner bloggers might charge as little as $5 per post, while a highly experienced blogger might charge $50 or more per post. Well-known bloggers with large, established online audiences might charge $100 or more to write a single blog post. The key is to find someone who can write in the style you want and understands your business and audience but can also work within your budget. The freelance websites listed earlier in this chapter are great resources for finding bloggers. You can also publish an ad for a blogger on ProBlogger (www.problogger.net) or the Freelance Writing Jobs Network (www.freelancewritinggigs.com), which are two popular blogs for bloggers and freelance writers, respectively.

QUICK TIP

When you hire a blogger, you need to determine if you want that blogger to use his or her name in the bylines published with posts on your business blog or if you want the blogger to ghostwrite posts for you. If bloggers' biographies on your business blog include links to the bloggers' own blogs and online profiles (which could drive a larger audience to those blogs), they might be willing to reduce their fees in exchange for the additional online exposure. It's something to consider as you're negotiating fees.

Creating Blogger Buzz

There is more to leveraging the world of blogging to boost your business than simply publishing your own content on your own business blog. You should also spend time trying to create blogger buzz about your business. The first step to driving blogger buzz is leaving comments on other blogs and adding to the conversations happening on those blogs. This is how you start to build relationships with the specific bloggers that you might want to reach out to for buzz requests in the future.

Once you've developed relationships with other bloggers, you can e-mail them when you have great news to share and ask them to help you spread the word. Don't just send global messages to large lists of bloggers. This is called blog blasting, and bloggers don't like it. In fact, it's a surefire way to put yourself on a blogger's blacklist. Instead, reach out with personal messages requesting help in creating a buzz, and be sure to reciprocate if they ask for your help in the future. You can also reach out to bloggers you don't already have relationships with, but be prepared for the response rate to be lower. The key to success is building a band of advocates who will help you spread the word when you need it and whom you'll help in return when the time comes.

Alternately, you can get traffic from other blogs to yours by placing ads on those blogs. The advertising rate on blogs is often very reasonable (unless you want to place an ad on one of the most highly trafficked blogs). If you search for blogs that are highly focused and whose visitors match your target audience, then you can ask whether that blog accepts ads. You can also search ad networks such as BuySellAds.com to find appropriate blogs on which to place your ads. In other words, you can even leverage the social Web using *traditional* marketing tactics to grow your business. This approach is discussed in more detail in Chapter 19.

Don't Forget to Protect Yourself

When you publish content on your business blog, the entire Internet audience can read it and comment on it. With that in mind, consider consulting an attorney to ensure you publish adequate legal disclaimers and policies on your blog such as terms and conditions of use and a privacy policy. The sample policies and disclaimers included in this section were not created by an attorney, but they can give you a place to start in creating your own.

Sample Blog Comment Policy

A comment policy is important for any blog because it sets expectations for what types of comments you will edit or delete. It's important to keep the conversation on your business blog on topic and away from personal attacks, obscenities, and other kinds of language that might offend some members of your audience. Following is a sample comment policy, which you can modify to fit your business blog:

> Comments are welcomed and encouraged on this site, but there are some instances where comments will be deleted or edited:
>
> 1. Comments deemed to be spam or potential spam will be deleted.
> 2. Including a link in a comment is permitted, but comments should be relevant to the post topic. Posts with excessive links, as determined by the blog owner and automated comment spam filter, will be edited or deleted.
> 3. Comments containing profanity will be edited or deleted.
> 4. Comments containing language or concepts that could be deemed offensive will be deleted.
> 5. Comments that attack another person individually will be deleted.
>
> The owner of this blog reserves the right to edit or delete any comments submitted to this blog without notice. This comment policy is subject to change at anytime.

Sample Business Blog Privacy Policy

A privacy policy for a business blog should explain what information (if any) you track, analyze, collect, or share, as well as what you do with that information. The following sample privacy policy is for a business blog that collects information for no other reason than to analyze site performance metrics. It is shown to help get you started in creating your own:

> We do not share personal information with third parties, nor do we store information we collect about your visit to this blog for use other than to analyze content performance through the use of cookies, which you can turn off at any time by modifying your Internet browser's settings. We are not responsible for the republishing of content from this blog on other websites or in other media without our permission. This privacy policy is subject to change at any time and without notice.

Sample Business Blog Terms and Conditions of Use

A "terms and conditions of use" policy is the catchall legal disclaimer for your business blog that is published to protect you from lawsuits related to the content you publish. Following is a sample statement of the terms and conditions of use for a business blog, which you can tweak to fit your blog:

> All content provided on this blog is for informational purposes only. The owner of this blog makes no representations as to the accuracy or completeness of any information on this site or found by following any link on this site and will not be liable for any errors, omissions, or delays in this information or any losses, injuries, or damages arising from its display or use. All information is provided on an as-is basis. These terms and conditions of use are subject to change at any time and without notice.

Also, you should include a line about the type of copyright protection your blog uses. If you hold any trademarks that are used on the blog, include a line that identifies your business as the owner.

Chapter 8

Microblogging

Microblogging hit the social Web scene in 2007 when Twitter debuted, but it didn't get wide recognition until 2008, when Twitter became the center of attention at the annual South by Southwest conference. During the event, a live demo of the new microblogging service captured everyone's attention. By 2009, Twitter had become an integral method of global communication, and businesses were starting to realize the potential that publishing 140-character updates could deliver in terms of generating brand awareness, recognition, and loyalty. In 2010, it seemed like every business was eyeing Twitter as the "it" tool for marketing.

The truth of the matter is simple. Twitter is easy to use, free to use, and fun. Once you create your business's Twitter profile, begin to follow some interesting Twitter users, and attract some followers of your own, you'll see firsthand that microblogging is an amazing way to share information, build relationships, and build your business both directly and indirectly.

What Is Microblogging, and Why Should Your Business Do It?

Microblogging is the process of publishing short updates online (typically 140 characters or less) using a tool like Twitter, Plurk, or Jaiku.

Twitter is by far the most popular microblogging application, so this chapter will focus on it as the tool where your business needs to be in order to leverage the marketing opportunities that microblogging offers. Take a look at the "Twitter Terminology" sidebar to familiarize yourself with some of the commonly used Twitter-related jargon.

Once you create a Twitter profile for your business, you can publish updates whenever you want and about any topic that you want. Of course, for a business Twitter profile, you should publish content that accurately reflects your brand image, while injecting some of your personality at the same time. Using Twitter, you can also share links to interesting Web pages in your updates, you can reply to other Twitter users publicly or privately, and you can retweet interesting updates published by other Twitter users.

An important aspect of effectively using Twitter is connecting with other users through Twitter's follow feature. When you follow another person on Twitter, that person's tweets appear in the stream of updates shown on your Twitter home page, so it's easy to read the thoughts of

TWITTER TERMINOLOGY

- **Tweet:** A message of 140 characters or less published to a user's Twitter profile.

- **Twitter stream:** A reverse-chronological archive of all of the tweets a user has published. The stream of tweets that appears in reverse chronological order on your Twitter home page includes all the tweets published by the people you follow.

- **Follow:** Agree to receive a Twitter user's tweets. When you sign up to follow someone on Twitter, that person's tweets show up in the Twitter stream on your Twitter home page, and your account name appears in the person's list of followers.

- **Retweet:** A tweet published by another person and shared with a user's own followers. If you like a tweet published by someone else on Twitter, you can retweet it by using the Retweet button provided in Twitter or by copying the original tweet and adding *RT* in front of it before you publish it to your Twitter stream.

- **@reply:** A phrase entered either at the beginning of a tweet to show it's directed to a specific Twitter user or within a tweet to mention another Twitter user.

people you're interested in connecting with. Likewise, when people follow you, your updates appear in their Twitter home page streams, making it easy for them to view and possibly retweet your interesting posts, putting you in front of their audiences of followers, too. That kind of exposure is invaluable in terms of building brand awareness and developing relationships with a broader audience online than you could ever get in the same amount of time on your own website. And remember, it's free!

Over the course of the past decade, consumers have been bombarded with more messages per second than they can possibly process. Businesses face the challenge of breaking through the clutter both online and offline to get their messages in front of consumers in a manner that enables consumers to actually notice and digest those messages. Furthermore, consumers don't have time to waste processing messages. Instead, they expect short messages that are to the point and easily absorbed. That's why Twitter is such a good fit for marketing communications. While a three-page direct-mail piece is

- **Direct message:** A private message one user can send to another. You can send direct messages only to people who already follow you.

- **Hashtag:** A keyword preceded by the # symbol in a tweet, entered to help Twitter users quickly find content related to a specific subject.

- **URL shortener:** An online application that allows you to enter a full URL for any specific Web page, click on a button, and automatically shorten that URL to an abbreviated version that is approximately 10 to 20 characters.

- **Twitter app:** Third-party-created applications that work with Twitter to enhance functionality and provide additional features.

- **Tweet chat:** A prearranged chat that happens on Twitter through the use of tweets that include a specific hashtag to link those tweets together in a virtual conversation.

- **Tweetup:** An in-person event where Twitter users meet, typically to network or socialize.

- **Live-tweet:** Attend an event and publish tweets throughout the event to share what's happening with your Twitter followers.

TRUE STORY

Some businesses thrive using Twitter as their only form of marketing. Seesmic launched as a startup with a nonexistent marketing budget and a Twitter account (@loic). Within a year, the company had over two million users. Crowdspring is another successful venture that does almost all of its marketing via its Twitter account (@crowdspring).

likely to end up in the garbage because recipients don't have time to read it, a 140-character tweet is easy to read.

In the 21st century, businesses have to find ways to create coveted brand relationships through the short communications that consumers respond to. By using a tool like Twitter and other social media marketing tactics, you can create branded experiences across the social Web. By focusing on creating experiences and joining the online conversation, you can create your own sound bites, giving them a chance to spread via an online buzz that lasts more than 140 characters.

In simplest terms, Twitter gives businesses the opportunity to meet these objectives:

- Monitor, listen to, and respond to the online conversations about their products, services, brands, customers, competitors, and industries
- Guide the online buzz about their businesses
- Deliver messages and information directly to online influencers
- Build relationships with a global audience
- Promote their products and services directly and indirectly

The bottom line is that Twitter offers businesses an incredible opportunity by allowing them to connect with large audiences and build relationships. If your customers are using Twitter (and chances are high that some of your customers are active on Twitter already), then you should be there, too. You can use Twitter as a business tool for a wide variety of purposes, such as marketing, customer service, recruiting, research, and more. Just as Dell's @DellOutlet Twitter account is highly successful in generating direct sales, Comcast's @ComcastCares Twitter account is excellent at providing customer service. In other words, Twitter can be used by multiple departments within a company for multiple purposes, but underlying all of those

THE COFFEE GROUNDZ FINDS SUCCESS WITH TWITTER

The Coffee Groundz is a retail coffee shop in Houston that is committed to promoting and supporting local businesses and working with those businesses to grow together. The Coffee Groundz uses its Twitter profile for that purpose and as a tool to conduct actual business and build relationships with existing and prospective customers.

For example, the Coffee Groundz was one of the first businesses to accept takeout orders via Twitter. In addition, the Coffee Groundz Twitter stream is filled with @replies, which shows that the company is truly trying to converse with people and build relationships with them. The Coffee Groundz also promotes upcoming events and tweetups that attract repeat and new customers each month. Overall, the company's Twitter stream offers a well-balanced mix of interesting content, conversations, and promotion.

efforts should be the goal of building relationships. For an example of how a small business can effectively leverage microblogging for sales and relationship building, see "The Coffee Groundz Finds Success with Twitter."

Twitter for Business Quick-Start Plan

Getting started with Twitter is extremely easy, and the Twitter for business quick-start plan provided in this section will help you become an active member of the Twitter community within minutes. As with all tools of the social Web, success won't come overnight. However, with patience and persistence, your network of followers will grow, relationships will develop, and your business will benefit from your efforts. Using books like *Twitter Power* by Joel Comm (Wiley, 2009) or *Twitter for Dummies* by Laura Fitton and Michael Gruen (Wiley, 2009) can help, but truthfully, Twitter really is a tool that you can learn through hands-on experimentation. To begin, follow these steps:

1. **Create your Twitter account:** Visit http://twitter.com, and select the Sign Up Now link to create your account. Provide the information requested, and be sure to take some time to pick the best Twitter user

name, because you can't change it later. Consider using your business name, blog or website domain name, or other branded identity that will represent your business online over the long term as your user name. Your Twitter ID will be known as @username where *username* is replaced with the user name you selected when you created your Twitter account. Choose wisely.

2. **Customize your Twitter profile:** Once your account is created, take some time to edit your account settings, as shown in Figure 8.1. Upload an image that identifies your business (called your *avatar*). Add a profile description that describes your business, as well as a link to your website or blog where you want people to find more information about your business. Also, take some time to customize your Twitter profile design by modifying the colors to match your brand and uploading a custom background image that matches your business. Resources for creating custom Twitter backgrounds can be found in Appendix B.

3. **Set up alerts:** Use a tool like TweetBeep (www.tweetbeep .com) to set up keyword alerts so you receive an e-mail when Twitter users tweet those keywords. Be sure to include your business name,

Figure 8.1 The Twitter profile settings page

your competitors' names, and any other keywords related to your business.

4. **Start tweeting:** Get your Twitter stream going, so if other Twitter users find your profile, you have some great content already available for them to view.

5. **Find people to follow:** Use the Find People feature in Twitter to find people you know and follow them. Take some time to see who they follow, and follow new people who seem to match your target audience. Also, use the Twitter advanced-search function to find people who are already tweeting about topics that include keywords related to your business, and then follow them. You don't have to have an existing relationship with a person to follow him or her on Twitter, so go ahead and follow people who seem to fit your business or simply because they're interesting.

6. **Join conversations:** Check out other Twitter streams and start retweeting and sending @replies.

7. **Feed your blog into your Twitter stream:** Use a tool like Twitterfeed (www.twitterfeed.com), which automatically publishes your blog's feed on your Twitter stream.

8. **Add follow badges and Twitter widgets to your blog site and other social media profiles:** Visit http://twitter.com/goodies to get tools to promote your Twitter stream on your blog, website, social media profiles, and anywhere else you can think of to boost your followers. You can also find tools from TwitterCounter (http://twittercounter.com).

9. **Keep tweeting:** The more active you are on Twitter (publishing tweets that add value), the more success you can have using Twitter as a tool to build your business.

 QUICK TIP

In addition to setting up alerts to monitor your business on Twitter, you can use Twitter's advanced-search option (http://search.twitter.com/advanced), which is shown in Figure 8.2, to conduct ad hoc searches and find conversations related to your keywords of choice. You can narrow your search to Twitter users in specific locations or tweets published within a specific time frame.

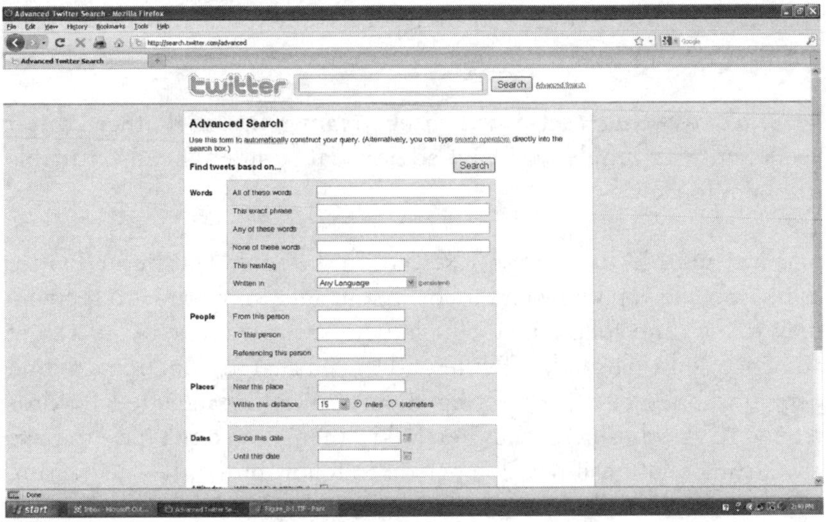

Figure 8.2 The Twitter advanced-search page

Types of Tweets

What should you tweet about on a business Twitter account? The honest answer is anything you want, as long as it's befitting of your brand message, image, and promise. You don't want to confuse or offend your followers, but you also want to be human and personable. It's up to you to find the balance that works for you and your audience. Just remember that the vast majority of your tweets should not be self-promotional if you want to be successful in using Twitter as a tool to build your business. To be safe, follow the 80-20 rule discussed in Part I.

Still, it can be hard for business owners to know what to publish about their business in 140 characters or less that followers will find interesting. You'd actually be surprised what people find interesting on Twitter! However, the following list of 15 easy tweet ideas can help you get past writer's block and start tweeting:

1. **What you're doing now:** Are you working on something interesting at this very moment? Tweet it.
2. **What you're going to do:** What's next on your agenda? Share it with your followers, so they get to know what your day is like.

3. **What you just finished doing:** Did you recently accomplish an interesting task or finalize a project? Tweet about it to your followers.
4. **Share content you like:** Share links to content you see online that you like. You can tweet links to articles, blog posts, videos, images, and more.
5. **Retweet tweets that you like:** If you read a tweet published by someone else that you want to share with your followers, retweet it.
6. **Ask a question:** Don't be shy. Ask away!
7. **Just for fun:** Did you see a movie you liked last night? Tweet it.
8. **Educational:** Tell your followers how to do something or lead them to educational information. Even a simple tip will do.
9. **Recommendations and reviews:** Have you tried a new product recently? Visited a new location? Read a new book? Tell people about it on Twitter.
10. **Likes and dislikes:** "I love my iPhone." A tweet truly can be as simple as that.
11. **Promotional updates:** Keep them to a minimum, but you can tweet about your business promotions, coupons, events, and so on.
12. **Respond to a tweet you like:** Send an @reply to someone in response to one of his or her tweets or to start a conversation.
13. **Acknowledge someone or something:** Did someone publish something online that you liked? Publish a tweet acknowledging the good work.
14. **Participate in Twitter events:** Livetweet an event, or join a TweetChat.
15. **Ponder the meaning of life:** Well, maybe not exactly, but you can publish random thoughts as tweets just because you're thinking them at the moment. (Just stay true to your followers' expectations for your business when you publish your random thoughts.)

The most important thing to remember as you're publishing tweets is this: Not every tweet has to be amazing, but you should always try to add value to the online conversation. Vary your tweets, keep your Twitter stream interesting, be engaging, and you'll see your list of followers grow and your success with it.

Quality vs. Quantity: The Truth About Twitter Followers

There is a widely held belief that it's important to get as many people to follow you on Twitter as possible in order to build your business. While it's true that a large audience of followers raises the chances that more people will see your content and share it with their audiences, giving you potential exposure to an audience you couldn't reach alone, using Twitter to build your business is truly about quality of followers, not quantity. Many people join Twitter and seek out as many people to follow as possible under the mistaken assumption that those people will reciprocate and follow in return. However, blindly following people who aren't interested in your business won't help you any more than untargeted advertising would.

It's better to have 1,000 highly interested followers than 10,000 followers who don't care about you or your tweets. Remember, the goal of social media marketing, including using Twitter as a marketing tool, is to build relationships, particularly with people who are invested in your business and are likely to become your advocates. In other words, tweeting to 10,000 people who ignore you is a waste of time, but tweeting to 1,000 people who find value in your tweets can lead to direct and indirect sales.

QUICK TIP

Notice the number of people a person follows compared with the number of followers that person has on Twitter. If a person follows far more people than follow him or her, it's likely that the person is trying to up the *quantity* of followers to appear popular on Twitter without much regard to the *quality* of those followers. In other words, don't just look at the numbers attached to Twitter profiles. Instead, review a person's Twitter stream to see if the person is actively engaging with others through retweets, @replies, and so on. Active, engaged people are the ones you want to connect with most on Twitter in order to build your business.

Don't be tempted to follow anyone and everyone on Twitter, and don't be swayed into thinking that Twitter profiles with large lists of followers are truly the most popular and powerful. Always think of quality over quantity when it comes to using Twitter as a marketing tool. Slow growth in quality Twitter followers trumps fast growth in quantity of Twitter followers when it comes to business growth that will last.

Must-Try Twitter Tools and Apps for Businesses

Twitter is an open-source application, which means the code used to create Twitter is available to the public. Developers use that code to create third-party applications (called Twitter apps) that can add features and enhance the functionality of Twitter. Some of the tools and apps that can help you make the most of Twitter have already been discussed throughout this chapter, including TweetBeep, Twitterfeed, Twittter widgets, TwitterCounter, and Twitter's advanced-search tool. It's easy to test new apps anytime to determine whether or not they'll add value to your Twitter experience.

Most Twitter apps are available free of charge, and the sheer number of available apps can be overwhelming. Following are a variety of apps that are particularly helpful to small and midsize businesses in terms of connecting with target audiences and marketing products and services:

- **TweetDeck:** TweetDeck (www.tweetdeck.com) helps you get organized and save time. When you download TweetDeck and associate your Twitter account with it, you can create groups of followers that appear in columns across your screen, so it's easier to keep track of tweets from separate audiences. You can tweet, retweet, reply, send messages, and so on directly from Tweet-Deck. Twitter apps offering similar features include HootSuite (www.hootsuite.com) and twhirl (www.twhirl.org).
- **Twitpic:** You can upload photos from your computer or mobile phone to your Twitpic (www.twitpic.com) account and then tweet them to your followers. Twitter apps offering similar features include yfrog (http://yfrog.com) and TweetPhoto (www.tweetphoto.com).
- **Monitter:** Use monitter (www.monitter.com) to get a real-time look at what people in your specified area are saying about the topics you determine by selecting relevant keywords. Twitter apps offering additional real-time information include TweetScan (www.tweetscan.com) and Twazzup (www.twazzup.com).
- **twtQpon:** You can easily create exclusive coupons to share with your Twitter followers using twtQpon (www.twtqpon.com).
- **TweetMeme:** TweetMeme (www.tweetmeme.com) is useful for tracking popular links as well as recent news from a variety

Figure 8.3 The TweetMeme Retweet button

of categories on Twitter. Additionally, you can get the popular Retweet button, shown in Figure 8.3, to publish on your blog or website and make it easy for people to tweet links to your blog posts. The button is available for download at http://tweetmeme .com/about/retweet_button. A similar button is offered by Twit-This (www.twitthis.com).

- **Twellow:** You can create your own listing on Twellow (www .twellow.com) similar to creating a listing in the yellow pages.
- **Localtweeps:** Search for Twitter users by zip code, city, or keyword on Localtweeps (www.localtweeps.com). You can also post local events to Localtweeps. Twitter applications offering similar "local" features include GeoFollow (www.geofollow.com) and ChirpCity (www.chirpcity.com).
- **Nearby Tweets:** To find tweets that reference a specific location, you can use Nearby Tweets (www.nearbytweets.com).
- **WeFollow:** Using WeFollow (www.wefollow.com), you can find Twitter users based on their interests, and you can list yourself using keywords and categories that are related to your business and that your target audience would be interested in.
- **Twtvite:** Twtvite (www.twtvite.com) allows you to invite people to an event and keep track of replies to your invitation.

- **ExecTweets:** ExecTweets (www.exectweets.com) is a directory of Twitter users who hold executive-level positions within their organizations. It's a great place to learn what leaders are tweeting about, and if you're an executive, it's a great place to get listed.

- **SocialOomph:** SocialOomph (www.socialoomph.com), formerly called TweetLater, offers a wide variety of free features and advanced features for a fee. One of the best free features is the ability to write tweets and schedule them to publish in the future. FutureTweets.com (www.futuretweets.com) offers a similar scheduling feature.

- **TwitterContd:** When 140 characters aren't enough, you can use TwitterContd (www.twittercontd.com) to tweet up to 1,250 characters. You can also use TwitterContd to upload and tweet pictures, video, and audio. TwitLonger (www.twitlonger.com) offers a similar feature.

- **BackTweets:** Since most Twitter users share links in tweets using a URL shortener, which disguises the original link, your monitoring efforts can miss some of the tweets that send traffic to your blog or Web pages. BackTweets (www.backtweets.com) translates those links and gives you a more comprehensive list of tweets that include links to your blog or Web pages.

- **Twimailer:** Twimailer (www.twimailer.com) is a great time saver. Using Twimailer, you receive more detailed e-mails when your Twitter profile gets new followers, including the new follower's location, following and follower statistics, and most recent tweets. Topify (www.topify.com) offers similar features.

- **FileTwt:** You can easily and quickly upload files of up to 20 megabytes and tweet them using FileTwt (www.filetwt.com).

- **Twitter Analyzer:** Twitter Analyzer (www.twitteranalyzer.com)

QUICK TIP

Twitter apps are created by third-party developers who may or may not decide to maintain them. Therefore, it's important to understand that Twitter apps can come and go. In fact, by the time you read this book, it's likely that new and improved apps have been introduced. Take some time to search for Twitter apps that appeal to you. A number of websites, including Twitdom (http://twitdom.com), offer lists and reviews of Twitter apps. You can even publish a tweet and ask your followers for suggestions!

provides a variety of statistics about your Twitter profile activity and performance, but you can't get complete information unless you submit your Twitter account information to the site. Other Twitter apps that offer analytical information include Twitter Grader (www.twittergrader.com), TweetStats (www.tweetstats .com), TweetReach (www.tweetreach.com), and Retweetist (www.retweetist.com).

Twitter Do's and Don'ts

You might remember that earlier in this chapter I said there is no wrong or right way to use Twitter, and that's absolutely true. It's a free and open platform that people can use in any way they wish, as long as they don't violate the terms of use defined by Twitter. However, if you're using Twitter as a marketing tool to build your business, you should follow some unwritten rules of use and etiquette to ensure your efforts are rewarded. The following do's and don'ts of Twitter behavior are some of the most important ones to adhere to if you want to achieve marketing success through microblogging.

Don't Overpromote

Twitter is a great place for self-promotion, but as you've already learned in this chapter, you shouldn't use it predominantly as a promotional tool. No one wants to listen to you talk about yourself all day. Stick to the 80-20 rule, and vary your tweets between nonpromotional and promotional, so your followers believe you're interested in more than selling your products and services.

Be Patient

Twitter offers an opportunity, not a guarantee, and it takes time to fully leverage that opportunity. For Twitter to deliver any kind of positive results for you, you need to be prepared to invest time in using it. Just as it takes time to build a reputation and relationships offline, the same holds true online, particularly when you're trying to do it in snippets of 140 characters or less.

Be Human

Show your personality through your tweets. If your Twitter stream is filled with corporate rhetoric, jargon, and buzzwords, then reading your tweets will be no more interesting than reading a company newsletter or brochure. No one wants to build a relationship or have a conversation with a scripted brochure.

Be Engaging and Interactive

Twitter should not be one-sided. Instead, your Twitter stream should show that you're involved in two-way conversations. Make an effort to engage other Twitter users by retweeting their updates and sending @replies and direct messages to them. If your Twitter stream isn't interactive, then it's probably boring and possibly too self-promotional.

Be Active and Varied

Twitter can't be an effective marketing tool if you're not actively using it, and I mean really actively using it. The more active you are with Twitter, the more chances you have to engage with other people, start conversations, and build relationships that lead to direct and indirect marketing opportunities. You also have to be varied in your tweets. Use the list of tweet suggestions earlier in this chapter to keep your Twitter stream interesting, and be sure to use Twitter apps to tweet content other than text, including images, audio, and video.

Add Value and Be Interesting

The most important thing you can do on Twitter is to share content and engage in conversations that add value to your audience members' lives. Whether you're sharing your expertise, answering a question, or simply offering your opinion, your content is essential to your Twitter success. If your content is filled with meaningless fluff that is either inconsequential or irrelevant to your business and target audience, then it won't help you build your business. Instead, focus on adding value and being interesting, just as you would if you started or joined a conversation in person.

Acknowledge and Promote Others

Since Twitter isn't one-sided and is all about building relationships, then it makes sense that you should spend time acknowledging other people and promoting other people and businesses through your tweets. If you see a great article, blog post, tweet, interview, or other content about a person you know is on Twitter, tweet about it, and be sure to include the person's user name within your tweet as an @reply to acknowledge his or her work. Similarly, if you hear of a great promotion or visit a business you really like, tweet about it (include the @reply if possible). Doing so not only is polite, but also puts you on the other user's radar screen. That person might send you an @reply to say thank you, which puts you in front of his or her entire audience of followers, too. The possibilities are endless!

Don't Get Too Personal or Negative

Your Twitter profile for your business should be public, which means anyone with Internet access can read your tweets. Therefore, your tweets should be human and show your personality, but they shouldn't be too personal. If you wouldn't share information with a customer in person, you shouldn't share that information on Twitter. Remember, your tweets can spread far beyond your audience of followers. Also, don't be tempted to be negative or publish overly critical tweets, which could land in front of the wrong eyes and come back to haunt you later. Be polite and be respectful.

Connect with Influencers

Once you have some tweets published and a group of followers, search for Twitter users in your industry who have powerful audiences

GETTING OTHERS TO TWEET ABOUT YOUR BUSINESS

One of the biggest coups in using Twitter for marketing is getting other Twitter users to tweet about your business. How do you do it? Well, there are several ways:

- Tweet useful, interesting, entertaining content that adds value to your audience.

- Offer valuable, exclusive deals and promotions that people want to share.

- Share their content first.

- Pay them by using a tool like Sponsored Tweets, which links Twitter users with advertisers (like your business) who want people to publish specific tweets. Other services that link advertisers with Twitter publishers in various ways include Twittad (www.twittad.com), Magpie (www.be-a-magpie.com), or BeTweeted (www.betweeted.com).

and are influencers both on Twitter and off. Use Twitter's advanced-search function and the Twitter apps listed earlier in this chapter to find people to follow, and then reach out to them via direct messages, retweets, and @replies to get on their radar screens. Invest time in building relationships with online influencers, so they're part of your own audience. If online influencers share your tweets or content, your message can spread far and fast. To learn more about persuading online influencers to tweet about your business, see "Getting Others to Tweet About Your Business."

Have a Plan

If tweeting doesn't come easy to you at first, don't despair. Create a plan for yourself, so you know what you want to accomplish each day. Set aside five minutes in the morning to read through your followers' tweets and send @replies and retweets. Set another five minutes aside in the middle of the day to search for new people to follow, and set aside five more minutes at the end of the day to tweet your own great content or promotions as well as to send more @replies and retweets. You can vary your plan from one day to the next, and soon you'll find that Twitter becomes a regular part of your day. You might even enjoy it and find you have to watch the clock so you don't spend too much time on Twitter each day!

Use Tools to Boost Efficiency

Use tools like TweetDeck or HootSuite to organize your Twitter activities. Try new Twitter apps to find ones that help you save time and increase productivity. Some great apps are listed earlier in this chapter. Also, if you have a smart phone, there are a variety of Twitter apps that work seamlessly with mobile phones to make it easy to tweet anywhere and anytime.

Integrate Your Efforts with Other Online and Offline Marketing Initiatives

Take some time to integrate your Twitter, blog, and social media accounts using tools like Twitterfeed and Twitter widgets. Cross-promote your efforts by including your Twitter address everywhere you can think of, including on your marketing materials, in ads, on your business card, in your e-mail signature, on your invoices, and so on. Make sure your Twitter profile is branded to match your overall business brand, and publish tweets that match your brand image and promise to avoid causing customer confusion. Fully integrating your marketing efforts and conveying a cohesive brand image and message will give your marketing plan a greater opportunity for success.

Hiring Someone to Tweet for You

If you don't have time to manage your own business Twitter account, you can recruit one or more employees to tweet for you, or you can hire a professional to tweet for you. Employees are the best alternative, because they understand your business. However, if you don't have an employee who can tweet for you, then you can hire a professional tweeter to maintain your Twitter profile for you.

You can find many professionals using the freelance websites listed in Chapter 7. The amount you need to pay a professional tweeter varies depending on how much time you expect him or her to spend working on your account each day. Typically, you'll be charged a monthly fee based on a specific amount of time the professional is expected to work each day, and you'll need to provide guidelines that outline your expectations in terms of how many tweets you require, when, what types, and so on. Expect to pay several hundred to several thousand dollars per month for a professional tweeter based on that person's experience and your time requirements.

Chapter 9

Social Networking

Social networking is just like the networking you do in person, but instead of dressing in a business suit and attending a cocktail party or seminar, you can use the tools of the social Web to network with people around the world from the comfort of your own home. Social networking tools like Facebook, LinkedIn, MySpace, Bebo, and others make it easy for you to create a profile where you can share information, communicate with people, upload photos and videos, and more. In fact, it's hard to believe that social networking hasn't been around for that long. The thought of being able to network with people only at in-person events seems incredibly limiting today. Thanks to social networking tools, hundreds of millions of people are within reach and available to connect with you as well as to hear and share your messages. It's an opportunity that a business owner would be crazy to ignore!

The two most popular social networking sites for business development are Facebook and LinkedIn. Therefore, this chapter focuses primarily on those tools, but you can find a list of other commonly used social networking sites in Appendix B. Keep in mind, it's important to grow your online presence in order to grow your business, so maintaining profiles on multiple social networking

QUICK TIP

You can create your own social network for a fee at www.ning.com.

sites where your target audience spends time is a good idea. However, don't spread yourself too thin. Success in social media marketing comes from quality, not just quantity.

What Is Facebook, and Why Should You Use It to Build Your Business?

Facebook (www.facebook.com) is used by over 350 million people, and it is by far the most popular social networking site in the United States. You can create a personal Facebook profile, a Facebook page for your business, and even a Facebook group for like-minded people to communicate in smaller niches. Facebook offers a variety of tools to enhance your profile, including third-party applications that can give you access to additional tools, but overall, customization features are fairly limited. Unlike a microblogging site like Twitter, Facebook is more private. You can see Facebook profiles only of people in your network of connections (called *friends*), and even public profiles can be viewed only by logged-in Facebook members. However, sites like Facebook continually modify privacy policies, so always be sure to read the current policies and configure your account according to your personal preferences.

Facebook is flexible in terms of how you can use it. While many of the apps available to use with Facebook allow users to play games with each other, you don't have to allow access to your profile from these apps. That means you can control the brand image of your Facebook profile by publishing focused content and engaging in activities and conversations that accurately reflect your brand promise. It might seem like a great idea to publish a video of that crazy frat party you went to in college, but do you really want your customers and business associates to see that video? If you want to use your Facebook profile as a business development tool, then you should forgo publishing that video or any other content or conversations that can detract from a user's engagement with your profile and perception of your brand.

QUICK TIP

Many social gaming apps are available on Facebook, but be careful which of these game apps you add to your Facebook profile. Not only can they clutter your Facebook wall, but they can also damage consumers' perceptions of your business and brand.

The same suggestion holds true for your business's Facebook page or group. What's the difference between Facebook profiles, pages, and groups? It's actually very simple.

Facebook Profile

A Facebook profile is an individual person's space on Facebook. Anyone who is connected to that person can comment on his or her Facebook wall, which is a stream of updates published by that person to his or her account. That person can upload a variety of media, participate in games, join groups, add pages to their list of likes, and more. Facebook users can also send messages to up to 20 friends at the same time. Your Facebook profile can be made public for anyone logged into Facebook to view, semiprivate so only parts of the profile are visible to anyone logged into Facebook, or completely private, meaning no one can view any part of your profile unless that person is a *friend* with you already.

Facebook Page

A Facebook page is a business's, brand's, organization's, or celebrity's space on Facebook. A valid representative for an entity can create a Facebook page and maintain it as the admin for that page. Any Facebook user can *like* a page (previously referred to as becoming a *fan* of that page) in order to be able to publish comments and participate in conversations through that page. The administrator can also upload images, videos, and more to the page as well as send update messages to everyone who has *liked* that page at once. Recipients cannot respond to these updates, but they can opt out of receiving them. Facebook page administrators also have access to a variety of statistics about the page's performance.

Facebook Group

A Facebook group can be created by any Facebook user and maintained by multiple administrators. Groups can be open for any Facebook user to join, or they can be closed, meaning a Facebook user needs to be invited or request permission to join the group. The group's admin can send messages to up to 500 members at the same time, and members can reply to the administrator's group messages. However, group members cannot opt out of group messages unless they leave the group. Group members can join in conversations, share content, and more. A group can be private, meaning the content is visible only to members, or it can be public, meaning any logged-in Facebook member can view the group's content.

What Should You Create on Facebook?

So should you create a Facebook profile, page, or group? The best-case scenario is that you have all of them, and possibly multiple niche groups. However, that's neither advisable nor intelligent when you

STEPS TO CREATE A FACEBOOK PAGE

1. Visit http://www.facebook.com/pages/create.php (shown in Figure 9.1), and select the appropriate categories for your official Facebook page. These settings should accurately reflect your business and can help Facebook members find your page in searches.
2. Type the name you want to call your Facebook page into the *Page name* text box. Take some time to choose the best name, because you can't change it later. You can use your business name or consider keywords that people would use to find a page like yours. The choice is yours.
3. Enter the provided security text, follow the links to read the Facebook policies related to pages, and click the *Create Page* button.
4. Next, take time to set up a great page by adding a profile picture that matches your business, such as your logo or your photo. Then enter information about your company, so new visitors know what you do and how you can help them. Don't forget to include your website's URL.
5. Click the *Publish* button, and your page goes live.
6. *Like* your page and send messages to your Facebook friends suggesting that they *like* your page, too. You can also conduct Facebook searches for people who might be interested in your business and send *like* suggestions to them.
7. Create amazing content, share interesting links, upload images, and turn your official page into an interesting, engaging source for people to visit. You can also provide exclusive content, discounts, and so on to people who have added your Facebook page to their list of *likes* to make them feel special and increase the number of people who *like* your page.

first get started with Facebook and social networking. For one thing, managing a profile, page, and group takes time. If you're not actively sharing content, starting conversations, and engaging other users, then creating a Facebook profile, page, and group won't help you. Instead of getting overwhelmed by all of the options Facebook offers, start small, and work in manageable chunks. In other words, start your personal profile page first, and assume that some of your clients, customers, and business associates will connect with you via that profile now or in the future. That means you should inject your personality into your Facebook profile but always consider the audience who

8. Promote your Facebook page by linking to it from your blog, other social networking profiles, your own Facebook profile, your Twitter profile, via e-mail to your address book, in your e-mail signature, and anywhere else you can think of. There are some tools which can help you with Facebook promotion; these are discussed later in this chapter.

9. Stay active and continually create interesting and useful content while interacting with people who *like* your page.

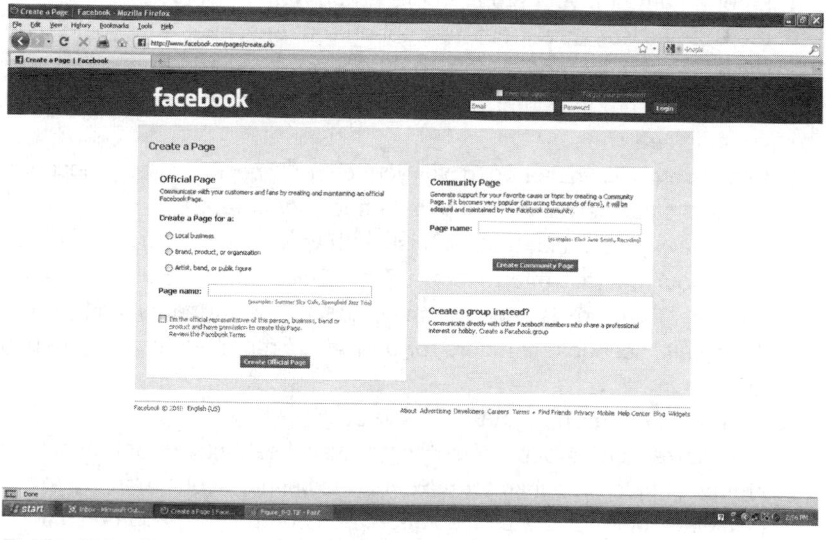

Figure 9.1 Create a new Facebook page.

might view your content to ensure it meets their expectations from you and your business.

Next, create a Facebook page for your business (see "Steps to Create a Facebook Page, on the previous spread"). Use your business name or keywords in your Facebook page name to help people find it through searches, and begin adding content to the page and inviting people to *like* the page.

As conversations develop and your friends and fans grow, you can create niche groups for further discussions (see "Steps to Create a Facebook Group"). In fact, your friends and fans might even create groups on their own, which you can join (you can join up to 300 Facebook groups). Take some time to search for groups related to your business where your target audience is already spending time,

STEPS TO CREATE A FACEBOOK GROUP

1. Log into your Facebook profile, and click the *Home* link in the top right navigation bar to ensure you're on the home page of your profile.
2. Select the *Groups* link in the left sidebar of your profile home page.
3. Click on the *Create a Group* button near the top center of the Groups page.
4. Enter a name for your group in the *Group Name* box (as shown in Figure 9.2), as well as a great description that describes who your group is for and encourages people to join. Keep keywords in mind as you create your group name; this will help Facebook members find your group in searches.
5. Use the drop-down menus to pick your *Group Type*. Pick wisely, because these choices can also help people find your group.
6. Enter news or an update to publish with your group when it goes live.
7. Enter your contact information in the *Office, Email, Website, Street*, and *City/Town* boxes. Keep in mind that this information will be visible to all Facebook members (or only group members if your group is private).
8. Click the *Create Group* button.
9. Customize your group by setting privacy settings (most business groups should be public for maximum exposure), configuring member privileges, uploading a profile image, and entering any additional information to set up your group the way you want it.
10. Invite your Facebook friends to become members of your group.

and then join those groups if they're open to new members and get involved in the conversations happening between group members.

All of your efforts to interact with people on Facebook and share your content and business news will work together to build your brand and your business. The more quality connections you have on Facebook, the more people you can share your messages with. If you're sharing amazing content, they're likely to take that content and share it further with their own connections. Social networking is an excellent indirect marketing tool, but many businesses have success using it as a direct-marketing tool, too. Just remember, try to stick to the 80-20 rule (at least 80 percent of your efforts nonpromotional and up to 20 percent self-promotional), so your time is spent building relationships rather than advertising and selling.

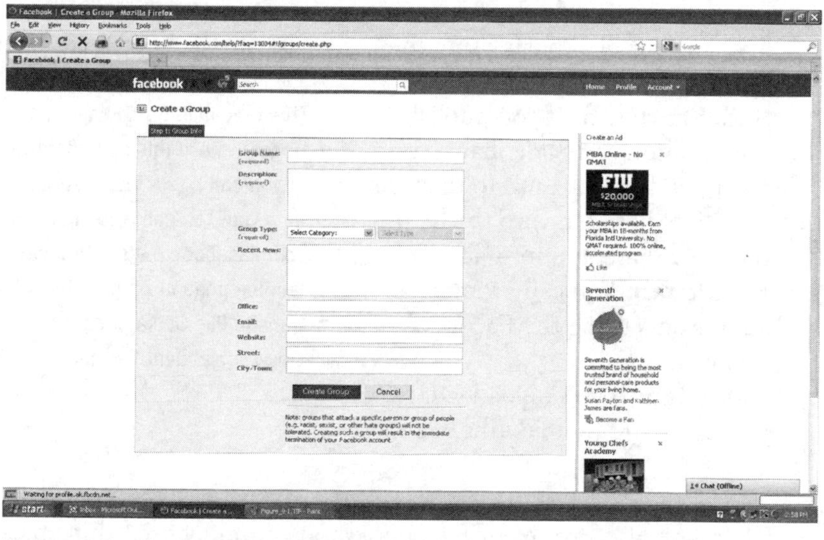

Figure 9.2 Create a Facebook group.

11. Publish some content to get the conversation going—updates, images, and so on. Be sure to stay active to keep your group engaging and interactive.
12. Promote your group on your Facebook profile, other social networking profiles, Twitter profile, blog, e-mail contacts, and so on.

Tools to Enhance Your Facebook Marketing Efforts

A variety of tools and features offered through Facebook can help you market your business directly and indirectly. Most of these tools help you share content and interact with other Facebook users, which makes sense, since social networking is just one more tool in your marketing toolbox to help you build relationships with a wider audience. The tabs that appear at the top of your Facebook profile can help people navigate through your profile easily. Several tabs for personal profiles are popular:

- **Blog tab:** You can showcase your own blog and blogs you like on this tab.
- **Notes tab:** You can automatically update your Facebook profile with links to your blog posts using the Notes tab features.
- **SlideShare tab:** If you publish presentations on SlideShare, you can provide quick links to them on the SlideShare tab with the help of the SlideShare app for Facebook.
- **Events tab:** You can promote your events using the Facebook Events tab.
- **Video tab:** If you upload videos, you can share them on the Video tab.

QUICK TIP

You can add custom tabs and a custom landing page to your Facebook page using the Static FBML application, which is available on Facebook. You need to know how to use HTML (the language for coding Web pages) to use this app effectively, or you can hire a Web developer to help you. You can also customize your Facebook page with a custom landing page or banner through a website like Social Identities (www.socialidentities.com).

There are also dozens of Facebook apps developed by third parties that can help you promote your business and share information on your business's Facebook page. Business applications can be found in the Facebook Applications Directory: http://www.facebook.com/?ref=home#!/apps/directory.php?app_type=0&category=100 (You must be logged into your Facebook profile to view the directory.) Some of the most popular apps for businesses include the following:

- **Marketplace:** With this app, you can sell, give away, buy, ask, or search for anything you want.
- **NetworkedBlogs:** Use this app to import your blog feed to your Facebook profile or page or to export your Facebook updates to your blog.
- **Eventbrite:** This app allows you to publicize events, sell tickets, and keep track of responses to your invitations.
- **My LinkedIn:** Use this app to add a tab to your Facebook profile or page that displays your public LinkedIn profile.
- **Promotions:** With this app, you can run branded promotions on your business's Facebook page, including contests, quizzes, and more.

You can set a personalized URL for your Facebook profile or page by visiting http://www.facebook.com/ username. Note that you cannot set a personalized URL for a Facebook page until that page has at least 25 people who have added it to their list of *likes*.

- **Payment E-Commerce Storefront:** If you want to be able to run a storefront, complete with payment processing, on Facebook, then this is a great app to use.
- **Memorable Web Addresses for Profile, Page, or Group:** With this app, you can create personalized URLs for your Facebook profile, page, and group. Not only are personalized URLs easier for people to remember, but they can also help people find you via searches.
- **Signup Form:** This app makes it easy to collect information from people via your Facebook page.
- **Social Tweet:** Feed your Facebook updates to Twitter and your Twitter updates to Facebook with this app.

Facebook also offers social plugins (http://developers.facebook .com/plugins) that allow you to connect the Facebook audience more closely to your website, blog, and so on. By copying and pasting a snippet of HTML code into your website or blog, Facebook social plugins will automatically connect your site to Facebook, making a personalized experience for each visitor. Several Facebook social plugins can enhance your marketing efforts:

- **Like button:** When you add the Like button to your website or blog, visitors can share pages from your site with their Facebook profile by simply clicking the mouse.
- **Comments:** This plugin enables visitors to publish comments on any piece of content on your website or blog.
- **Like box:** The Like box allows visitors to *like* your Facebook page and view its stream of updates without leaving your website or blog where the plugin is installed.
- **Activity feed:** When this plugin is installed on your site, visitors can see what their Facebook friends are doing on your site through likes and comments.
- **Facepile:** The Facepile plugin displays pictures of a visitor's Facebook friends who have already signed up for your site.
- **Login with Faces:** This plugin displays pictures of a visitor's Facebook friends who have already signed up for your site, as well as a Facebook log-in button.
- **Recommendations:** When this plugin is installed on your website or blog, visitors automatically see personalized suggestions for other pages on your site or blog that they might like.
- **Live Stream box:** As the word *live* implies, this plugin enables visitors to your website or blog to share comments and activities as they happen during a live event.

QUICK TIP

Common questions about Facebook social plugins are answered in the Facebook Help Center at http://www.facebook.com/help/?page=1068.

Using Facebook Ads for Added Exposure

Facebook offers an advertising service that has a price attached to it but could be worthwhile to test in an effort to increase the number of fans your Facebook page has. You can also create ads to promote events on Facebook. You can create ads using your own text and images, and you can target who will see your ads based on location, occupation, and a variety of other demographic criteria. Ads are displayed to users who meet your criteria.

When you create a Facebook ad, you determine how high you'd like to bid for space to display your ad. Facebook uses your ad-targeting

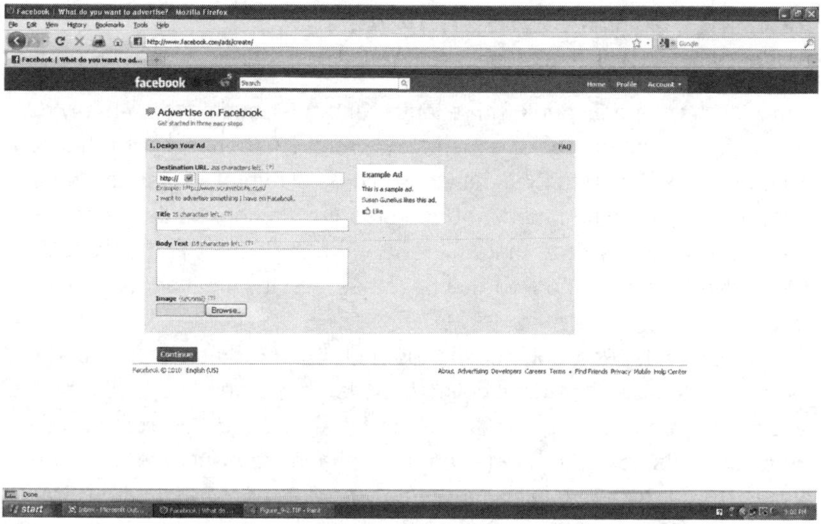

Figure 9.3   Advertise on Facebook.

criteria and your maximum bid price to serve ads to Facebook users. You can set up your ad so you either pay whenever someone clicks on your ad (pay per click) or whenever your ad is served (pay per impression). You can control your budget, so the risk is limited.

To create an ad on Facebook, simply click on the Advertising link at the bottom right side of any Facebook page. The Facebook Advertising page opens. Next, click on the Create an Ad button near the top right of your screen to open the Advertise on Facebook page (shown in Figure 9.3), where you can enter the text for your ad and upload your ad image. Once your ad is set up, you can set your budget and configure your targeting criteria. Facebook offers a variety of reports to help you track the performance of your ads, and you can make changes at any time in order to maximize the return on your investment.

Facebook for Business Quick-Start Plan

Many large and small companies have succeeded at building their businesses through Facebook. For an example, check out the sidebar "Red Bull Connects with Target Audience via a Facebook Page." You

RED BULL CONNECTS WITH TARGET AUDIENCE VIA A FACEBOOK PAGE

Red Bull is an energy drink with a large consumer audience primarily comprising teens and college-age men and women. To connect with this audience on Facebook, Red Bull knew it would be a mistake to simply publish company news and information. Understanding its core audience, Red Bull created a Facebook page that offers interesting content and entertaining, interactive features. The Red Bull page has over two million fans, and it's an active place.

For example, Red Bull doesn't just pull its corporate Twitter feed into its Facebook page. Instead, it collects feeds from several popular athletes. Additionally, entertaining content keeps fans engaged. An example is the Drunkish Dials box, where fans can rate calls made by people who "drunk-dialed" the 1-800-Red-Bull phone number, or the Procrastination Station box, which offers games dubbed "magnificent ways to waste some of your precious time." Even the posts made by the Red Bull team on the page are written in a language the target audience will respond to. For example, a March 2010 update stated, "Red Bull is stoked that Danny MacAskill is on the team!"

If you want to check out a big brand that is effectively connecting with its target audience through Facebook, Red Bull is one to watch at http://www.facebook.com/redbull.

can do it, too. Follow these steps to jump-start your Facebook marketing efforts today:

1. Create a comprehensive Facebook profile, and begin adding great content and friending other Facebook members. Be sure to get your personalized Facebook URL.
2. Feed your blog and Twitter stream to your Facebook profile, and add any other apps or tabs that increase the value of your profile.
3. Create a comprehensive Facebook page, and begin adding valuable content to it.
4. Feed your blog and Twitter stream to your Facebook page, and add any other apps or tabs that increase the value of your page.
5. Send invitations to *like* your page to your Facebook friends, and search for other people who might be interested in your page. You can also send an e-mail to people in your e-mail address book, inviting them to *like* your page.

6. Promote your Facebook profile and page on your blog, other social networking profiles, Twitter, e-mail signature, and anywhere else you can think of to draw attention to them. You can also place Facebook ads to promote your page.
7. Use Facebook social plugins such as the Like button, Activity feed, and comments to increase interactivity and connectivity between your website, blog, and Facebook.
8. Consider creating niche Facebook groups related to your business, and invite people to become members. Create interesting content that encourages members to interact.
9. Don't give up. Your Facebook profile, page, and group need to stay fresh, or they'll stagnate and won't help your marketing efforts at all.

These steps provide a very general overview of how you can quickly develop your business's Facebook presence, so you can begin using Facebook as a marketing and relationship-building tool. Remember, content trumps all, so continually strive to publish amazing content to your Facebook profile, page, and groups. That content can come in the form of tips, links, discussions, images, videos, and more. As long as your audience finds your content useful or entertaining, you're on the right track to building your business through Facebook.

Getting Started with LinkedIn to Build Your Business

LinkedIn (www.linkedin.com) boasts over 65 million members with a common goal: social networking for business purposes. Therefore, LinkedIn is known as an excellent tool for business-to-business marketing. However, businesspeople are consumers, too, so it stands to reason that business-to-consumer marketing can be successful on LinkedIn as well. The commonly held belief is that Facebook is the better choice for business-to-consumer marketing, but each business needs to experiment to find the best social sites to connect with its target audiences.

LinkedIn is far more "closed" than Facebook. You need to have an established relationship with a LinkedIn member in order to connect with him or her. If you haven't worked in the same company or attended the same school, and don't know his or her e-mail address, then you might need to request an introduction through a LinkedIn

Figure 9.4   Create your LinkedIn profile.

member already connected to you and the person you wish to reach. To actively participate in the LinkedIn community, you need to create a personal LinkedIn profile (like the example shown in Figure 9.4). If you're using LinkedIn as a tool to market your business through relationship building, then your LinkedIn profile should be made visible to the public in order to increase your online exposure. Once your profile is active, you can leverage the various tools and applications offered through LinkedIn to directly and indirectly promote your company, products, and services.

> **QUICK TIP**
>
> Create a personalized URL for your LinkedIn profile by logging into your LinkedIn account, selecting the Profile link in the top navigation bar, and then clicking the Edit Profile link in the drop-down menu. Click the Edit link to the right of Your Public Profile, and enter a unique, personalized extension for your LinkedIn URL.

Of course, networking with other users and interacting with them is the most important thing you can do on LinkedIn, so you should take the time to search for people to connect with, using your own contact list and the LinkedIn search function. You can also use the Recommendations feature accessible through your LinkedIn profile to write and publish recommendations for people you're connected to and request that they write recommendations for you, too. Recommendations are published with your LinkedIn profile and serve as written testimonials and endorsements about you and your business. People trust reviews and recommendations from others, so building your list of recommendations can significantly increase your credibility and trustworthiness among the LinkedIn audience.

You should also add your Twitter feed to your LinkedIn profile, so your LinkedIn status automatically updates each time you publish a new tweet. You can easily add your Twitter feed to your LinkedIn account by selecting the Edit My Profile link once you're logged into your LinkedIn account, and then clicking the Add Twitter Account link, where you can enter your Twitter profile URL and configure settings for publishing your tweets on LinkedIn. It just takes a few seconds but adds a lot to your LinkedIn efforts by keeping your content fresh and engaging.

Using LinkedIn Groups and LinkedIn Answers to Promote Your Business

Two of the most useful features of LinkedIn for indirectly marketing your business are LinkedIn Groups and LinkedIn Answers. Both features give you the opportunity to connect with targeted audiences and share your expertise, which leads to stronger relationships and word-of-mouth marketing about you and your business.

LinkedIn Groups

When you join LinkedIn, you should search existing groups by clicking on the Groups link in the top navigation bar of your profile, and then selecting Groups Directory from the drop-down menu. From here, you can search for groups based on category, language, or keywords. When you find groups where your target audience is likely to participate, click through and analyze those groups. Find the ones that are most active and best targeted to your business, and join them. You can join up to 50 LinkedIn Groups (and additional subgroups).

Once you join a group, join the conversation. Get to know the other group members by actively participating in the group. You can even feed your blog updates to groups that enable the News Feeds option. The feature can be found under the News tab in "Latest

News" in groups where it's available. Just add your blog's RSS feed URL, and the group news will automatically display a link to your new blog post each time you publish one.

You can also start a LinkedIn Group if you can't find an existing group that meets your needs or if you have enough connections to draw other LinkedIn users to join your group (see the sidebar "Steps to Create a LinkedIn Group"). Once your group is created, invite people to join it, and make sure it's active. Don't forget to feed your blog updates into your own group.

STEPS TO CREATE A LINKEDIN GROUP

1. From your LinkedIn account home page, select the Groups link from the top navigation bar and then the Create a Group link from the drop-down menu.
2. Upload a logo or image to identify your group.
3. Enter a group name, category, summary, and description of your group. Take your time to pick a group name that is relevant. Consider using keywords so people can find your group when they conduct group searches on LinkedIn. Also, be sure to create a well-written, comprehensive summary and description, so people understand what your group is for and are enticed to join.
4. Connect your group to your business website by including the URL for your website in the text box labeled Website.
5. Your e-mail address is required, and the e-mail box is automatically filled with the e-mail address associated with your LinkedIn account.
6. Configure your group's access and privacy settings. First, choose whether you want any LinkedIn member to be able to join the group or if you need to approve someone's request to join before that person can become a member. (If you're trying to promote your business with your LinkedIn group, allowing anyone to join increases your online exposure.) To ensure that the most people possible have a chance to learn about your group, make sure "Display this Group in the Groups Directory" is checked. You should also make sure to check the box next to "Allow group members to display the logo on their profiles. Also, send my connections a Network Update that I have created this group," so group members can hear about your group and help you promote it. If you have employees or colleagues with the same e-mail domain who you want to be preapproved to join your group, enter those domains in the text box provided.

7. Choose the language for your group. If it's based in a single geo-graphic location, make sure the appropriate check box is checked.

8. Click the link to read the Terms of Service, and then select the check box stating that you read the policy.

9. Click the Create Group button.

10. Once your group has been created, you can invite people to join, begin adding content, feed your blog updates to your group's news, and so on.

11. Promote your LinkedIn Group on your LinkedIn profile, other social net-working profiles, Twitter profile, blog, with e-mail contacts, and so on.

12. Stay active and continually offer fresh content and conversation in your group so joining it is worthwhile. Active groups that provide useful information are typically much more successful than groups that just regurgitate company information, as demonstrated by the story in the sidebar about SafeNet.

SAFENET GENERATES $1 MILLION
FROM LINKEDIN IN ONE YEAR

SafeNet is one of the largest providers of information security solutions in the world. When Holger Schulze, director of product market and market-ing operations, started a LinkedIn group—the LinkedIn Information Secu-rity Community Group—as an experiment, he never expected it to grow to over 50,000 members in less than two years. But that's exactly what happened. In time, four SafeNet employees took the lead in sharing useful information and interacting with members of the group. They each spend a few hours per week on LinkedIn, and in 2009, those efforts directly led to $1 million in sales.

Interestingly, SafeNet created a second LinkedIn group called the SafeNet Group, which offered company news and information. That group attracted very few members, in stark contrast to the success of the information-sharing group. SafeNet didn't view the effort as a failure. Instead, the company turned the SafeNet Group into an internal group and walked away, having learned an important lesson: people aren't interested in groups that simply self-promote and talk about the company behind the group, but they are very interested in joining and participating in groups that offer information and conversations about subjects they enjoy or find valuable.

Figure 9.5   LinkedIn Answers

LinkedIn Answers

LinkedIn offers a unique and extremely useful tool with LinkedIn Answers. You can access LinkedIn Answers by logging into your LinkedIn profile and selecting the More link in the top navigation bar, and then clicking the Answers link in the drop-down menu. The LinkedIn Answers home page, shown in Figure 9.5, includes a space for you to ask a question and links that help you find questions you can answer.

The LinkedIn Answers feature provides a great opportunity for you to share your expertise, as well as the chance to find people who are asking questions related to your business or products and directly answering them. Whether a question is specifically about your company or about your industry doesn't matter, because both types of questions allow you to get your business name in front of an audience that is actively looking for the information you have. For example, you can click on the Advanced Answers Search tab and search for questions based on the keywords and categories you choose. You can even filter your results to include only unanswered questions. The potential to reach people who have already expressed some level of interest in your industry or business by publishing a question about it is incredible.

Tools to Help You Market Your Business Through LinkedIn

In addition to LinkedIn Groups and LinkedIn Answers, a variety of tools and applications can help you market your business via LinkedIn. Some apps offer direct-marketing opportunities, while others are valuable indirect-marketing tools. Don't be afraid to test different tools and applications. They certainly can't hurt your business!

Following are some popular LinkedIn apps for marketing your business:

- **Blog Link:** The Blog Link application makes it easy for you to import your blog's feed into your LinkedIn profile.
- **Events:** The Events app is incredibly useful in helping you spread the word about your business-related events. You can also see the events your connections are attending.
- **SlideShare Presentations:** You can share the presentations that you upload to SlideShare within your LinkedIn account.
- **Google Presentation:** You can share the presentations you have created with or uploaded to Google Apps in your LinkedIn profile.
- **Polls:** You can use the Polls app to conduct surveys and gather market research information. Advanced polling features are available for a fee.
- **Tweets:** With the Tweets app, you can display your tweets within your LinkedIn profile, and you can view your connections' tweets. You can also publish tweets without leaving LinkedIn.

QUICK TIP

You can get access to more features by paying a monthly fee to upgrade your LinkedIn account. Don't pay for an account when you sign up for LinkedIn. For most people, the free account is adequate. Take some time to use LinkedIn and better understand your activities, needs, and goals before you start paying for extra features.

Promoting Your Business with LinkedIn Ads

LinkedIn Ads allow you to directly advertise your business to LinkedIn members. Your LinkedIn ad can include a headline, text, and a link to your website. Ads automatically include a link to your LinkedIn profile as well. You can also select targeting criteria to ensure your ad is displayed to the right people, and you can choose the pay-per-click or pay-per-impression payment method. Along with your preset budget, you can control your spending. It's best to start small with LinkedIn advertising, so you can view your ad's performance, tweak it, and analyze whether it's worth the investment for your business before you spend too much money on it.

LinkedIn for Business Quick-Start Plan

Follow these steps to establish your presence on LinkedIn and market your business:

1. Create a comprehensive personal LinkedIn profile, and begin adding great content.
2. Send connection requests to people you know on LinkedIn. Be sure to search for people, too.
3. Feed your blog and Twitter updates to your LinkedIn profile, and add any other apps or tabs that increase the value of your profile.
4. Write recommendations for people you're connected to, and request that they write recommendations for you.
5. Use the reshare feature to share interesting content on LinkedIn.
6. Search for questions to answer using LinkedIn Answers, and answer questions related to your business or industry.
7. Search for groups related to your business and industry where your target customers already spend time, and join those groups. Feed your blog updates into the News feature of groups you belong to when the feature is enabled.
8. Create your own LinkedIn group for your business, and add useful content. Feed your blog to your group's news, and invite people to join your group.

QUICK TIP

Take a moment to read through the do's and don'ts of using Twitter and tips for hiring someone to tweet for you that were discussed in Chapter 8, because they apply to social networking, too.

9. Promote your LinkedIn profile and group on your blog, social networking profiles, Twitter profile, through e-mail, and any other way you can.
10. Consider placing LinkedIn ads to promote your business.
11. Stay active and make sure your LinkedIn profile and group participation are engaging and fresh.

How to Increase Your Social Networking Connections

While it is absolutely true that your social networking connections will grow organically over time as a result of your active participation across the social Web, you can speed the process up through promotion. Remember, truly building your business through social networking depends more on quality of connections than quantity, but it never hurts to connect with more people. Fortunately, you can use a variety of easily implemented methods and tools to increase your social networking connections. Several popular and effective methods follow:

- **Twitter:** Tweet about your social networking groups, profiles, and so on.
- **Buttons:** Include buttons on your blog and website that link directly to your social networking profiles, pages, and so on. Several websites where you can find free buttons to promote your social networking profiles are listed in Appendix B.
- **Ads:** Place ads online and on Facebook or LinkedIn.
- **E-mail:** Include links to your profiles, pages, groups, and so on in your e-mail signature line.
- **Widgets:** Some social networking sites offer widgets that you can add to your website or blog to promote your profiles, pages, groups, and so on. For example, you can add a Facebook badge to your blog or website to promote your Facebook page. Take some time to search for tools and widgets offered by the social networks you use for help in promoting your profiles across the Web. Facebook badges can be found at http://www.facebook .com/badges, and LinkedIn widgets can be found at http:// developer.linkedin.com/community/widgets.

- **Plugins:** Use the Facebook social plugins to increase the connectivity and interactivity of your website, blog, and so on with the Facebook audience.
- **Offline:** Don't forget that you can promote your social networking profile, pages, groups, and so on through your traditional offline marketing initiatives, too.

The bottom line is that you should try to increase your social networking connections anytime you can. For example, it never hurts to add a line to your e-mail messages or business card that says, "Connect with Me on LinkedIn" or "Join the ABC Business Facebook Group" with a link to your social networking accounts.

Chapter 10

Social Bookmarking and Content Sharing

One of the most powerful aspects of the social Web is the ability to share amazing content. Instead of publishing an article, image, or video on your business website and hoping you can drive traffic to that content, the social Web creates a way for people from around the world to share content they enjoy with bigger audiences than a business could ever reach on its own. Some social Web content-sharing tools allow you to upload your own content for further sharing *and* share content uploaded by other people. Other tools simply allow you to share links with comments about the content you like. Both types of tools can help you promote and grow your business, as this chapter describes.

What Are Social Bookmarking and Content Sharing, and Why Should Your Business Participate?

Content sharing is the process of sharing links (and often opinions or commentary) to online content that you think other people would be interested in, too. You can share content using a variety of tools described later in this chapter. Sometimes content sharing is limited to a niche audience of individuals who are connected on the social

Web, and other times, content sharing can be open to all Internet users to view and share further.

Social bookmarking is a specific type of content sharing that allows users to save and store online information or Web pages for future reference. Rather than adding Web pages to your Web browser's local Favorites menu, you can bookmark those pages using a social bookmarking tool, so you can access them from any computer with Internet access at any time. Social bookmarking becomes social when your shared content is visible to other people who use the same social bookmarking tools that you do. Some social bookmarking sites allow users to leave comments on shared content, rate shared content, and even share it further with their own audiences. In other words, social bookmarking becomes *social* when people discuss each other's shared content and share it further.

The fact that content sharing and social bookmarking allow people to interact and spread content across the Web means they offer significant opportunities for businesses to spread messages and build relationships with target audiences. In other words, sharing and bookmarking content on the social Web can raise awareness of your brand, boost brand loyalty, and even increase direct and indirect sales. As with most marketing tools of the social Web, content sharing and social bookmarking are long-term growth strategies that require patience and persistence. You need to listen, interact, and share content that adds value to user experiences in order to succeed in growing your business through content sharing and social bookmarking.

Popular Social Bookmarking Tools

There are many social bookmarking sites, and you can find a list of popular sites in Appendix B. However, the two most popular social bookmarking sites for building Web traffic and your business are Digg and StumbleUpon. Both sites offer slightly different advantages, and since most social bookmarking sites are fairly similar in terms of functionality, Digg and StumbleUpon are the best two sites for beginning your social bookmarking efforts.

Digg

Digg (www.digg.com) is by far the most popular social bookmarking site. In fact, Digg refers to itself as a social news site rather than a social bookmarking site, because the sharing and discussion features have virtually usurped the simple bookmarking feature. With Digg, you can find links to content that interests you and share content you like. In simplest terms, you submit (or *digg*) content you want to share by logging into your free Digg account and completing the content submission form, which includes a field for you to enter the content URL, a description, a category, and an image. Each submission is visible to all Digg users (whether or not they are actually members). Other Digg members can digg your submission (meaning they like it) or *bury* your submission (meaning they don't like it). Submissions that get a lot of diggs appear on Digg's home page and Popular Articles list, shown in Figure 10.1, where they can get a lot of exposure, traffic, and additional sharing.

You can comment on Digg submissions, too, and this is where Digg becomes social. Also, you can add friends to your Digg network to further interact with people. As you build relationships with your friends, you can help promote each other's content and drive additional exposure to your content. However, it's important to be realistic in setting your goals for using Digg as a tool to grow your business, because many users complain that Digg is controlled by a handful of top users who are able to push content to the top, leaving little hope for other content to get noticed. That doesn't mean you should avoid

Figure 10.1 Popular articles on the Digg home page

using Digg, though. Focus on building your network of targeted friends and submitting amazing content, and you'll see success in time.

StumbleUpon

StumbleUpon (at www.stumbleupon .com) works very similarly to Digg and other social bookmarking sites in that once you create a free account, you can submit content (or *stumble* it) to the StumbleUpon site, where other users can give it a thumbs up if they like it or a thumbs down if they don't like it. You can use your network of friends to help you promote your content, and content that becomes popular can drive a lot

QUICK TIP

Social bookmarking communities frown on sharing your own content. That doesn't mean you can never submit your own content to social bookmarking sites. As with all social media marketing plans, use the 80-20 rule: spend far more time submitting and promoting content from other people than you do submitting your own content. Also, be sure to promote content from people within your network and outside of your network so your activity does not appear biased.

of traffic to the source. The handy StumbleUpon toolbar that works with most Web browsers makes it incredibly easy to stumble content with the click of a mouse. Just complete the submission form shown in Figure 10.2, add a great title and description, choose a category for your submission, and you're done.

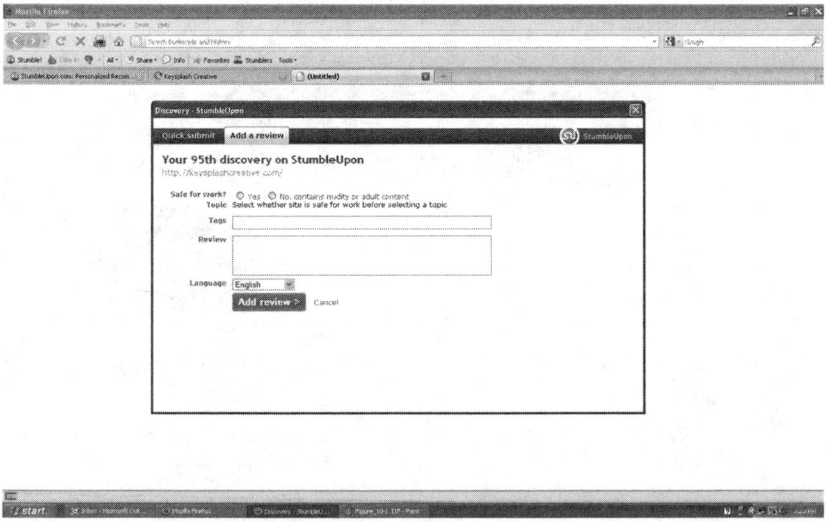

Figure 10.2 The StumbleUpon content submission form

StumbleUpon can drive a lot of traffic to your content, and that flow of traffic can last for quite a while. Just be sure to submit a variety of great content and interact with other users to build your reputation over time. Doing so will make your StumbleUpon efforts even more successful in the long term.

QUICK TIP

Take the time to create great titles and descriptions for the content you submit through social bookmarking to encourage people to click through and read the actual content at its source. Also, write titles and descriptions with keywords in mind to help people find your submitted content through searches.

Social Bookmarking for Business Quick-Start Plan

You can get started with social bookmarking within minutes and begin sharing content and making connections. Social bookmarking sites are typically free to use and registration is easy.

1. Create a Digg account.
2. Create a StumbleUpon account, and download the StumbleUpon toolbar for your Web browser.
3. Begin looking at the type of content people are already sharing on Digg and StumbleUpon to get an idea of what content is popular and to find people sharing the type of content you and your target audience would be interested in.
4. Friend other users who share content that is similar to yours and that your target audience would enjoy.
5. Digg and stumble other users' interesting content, and leave comments on submitted content that you enjoy.
6. Digg and stumble content you want to share, as well as some of your own amazing content, but always submit far less of your own content than content created by other people.

Popular Content-Sharing Tools

A wide variety of tools allow you to upload and share your own content or share content uploaded by other people. You can upload and share photos, videos, articles, presentations, and more. Content-sharing sites allow you to network with other users, share their content further, and even discuss content, creating a very social atmosphere. If you upload and share amazing content, it's likely to get noticed by your core audience and spread to their audiences, too. That sharing leads to more exposure for your business.

Following are details about some of the most popular tools for sharing different kinds of content via the social Web. You can find many more content-sharing sites listed in Appendix B. Additionally, video- and audio-sharing sites are discussed in Chapter 11.

Flickr

Flickr (www.flickr.com) is the most popular photo-sharing site, and many businesses have successfully used it to market their brands. For one such example, see the sidebar "Lay's Chips Finds Marketing Success Through Flickr." In simplest terms, you can submit your own photos, images, screenshots, and so on to Flickr. You can interact with other users by connecting with them as friends, and you can even join (or create your own) groups for niche sharing. You can configure privacy settings on your account to manage who can view your uploaded images, but for business users, it's best to keep your content public for maximum exposure. However, that means you need to make sure the only content you upload and share is appropriate for your business and brand.

LAY'S CHIPS FINDS MARKETING SUCCESS THROUGH FLICKR

In March 2010, Frito-Lay launched a social media marketing initiative leveraging the power of photo sharing via Flickr. The company created a branded Flickr page for Lay's chips, and people were invited to upload photos of themselves or people they know enjoying happy moments in their lives as part of "The Happiness Exhibit." Some of the photos will appear in an upcoming issue of *People* magazine and on the backs of Lay's packages.

The marketing campaign was promoted through ads and spreads in magazines like *People*, on packages of Lay's chips, and on websites like Facebook, iVillage, Yahoo!, YouTube, and Hulu. The integrated marketing effort drew attention from the social Web community quickly as word spread and more people uploaded their photos to the Lay's Flickr page. In less than one month, nearly 10,000 photos had been uploaded and shared on the Lay's Flickr page.

Additionally, consider applying a Creative Commons Attribution license to your uploaded images, so people can republish them on their own blogs and websites as long as they attribute you as the source. (To learn more about Creative Commons licenses, see "An Introduction to Creative Commons.") You should also be sure to read the Flickr guidelines and be cognizant of copyright restrictions, so you're sure you don't violate any site rules or copyright laws when you upload content. You can learn more about copyrights in Chapters 7 and 20.

AN INTRODUCTION TO CREATIVE COMMONS

Creative Commons licenses (www.creativecommons.org) were created to make it easier for people to share their published work than strict copyright laws allow. Any published work is automatically copyright-protected, which means you cannot republish it without obtaining permission from the copyright owner. There is a gray area of the law related to fair use that says content can be republished for educational purposes or news reporting, but it's safest to assume you can't republish text, images, or audio or video content unless you have permission to do so or the work has a copyright license attached to it that allows you to reuse It without obtaining permission. Creative Commons provides such a license.

Six types of Creative Commons licenses can be applied to your work. In the following list, the types are presented in order from least restrictive to most restrictive:

1. **Attribution:** Anyone can republish the work in any form as long as the original source is attributed.
2. **Attribution noncommercial:** Anyone can republish the work in any form as long as the source is attributed and the work is not used for commercial purposes.
3. **Attribution no derivatives:** Anyone can republish the work in the exact format as the original work as long as the original source is attributed.
4. **Attribution no derivatives noncommercial:** Anyone can republish the work in the exact format as the original work as long as the original source is attributed and the work is not used for commercial purposes.
5. **Attribution share alike:** Anyone can republish the work as long as the original source is attributed and the new work is licensed under the identical terms of the originally licensed work.

6. **Attribution share alike noncommercial:** Anyone can republish the work as long as the original source is attributed, the new work is licensed under the identical terms of the originally licensed work, and the new work is not used for commercial purposes.

When you upload and share your original content online, consider applying a Creative Commons Attribution license to it, because that license offers the biggest opportunity for your content to spread further and indirectly promote your business while still crediting you as the original publisher.

SlideShare

SlideShare (www.slideshare.net) is a website where users can upload their presentations in PowerPoint, PDF, or Word format and make them available for sharing by enabling functions for people to e-mail the presentations, print them, or embed them in their own blogs or websites. You can even add audio to your presentations to turn them into webinars (online seminars). Figure 10.3 shows an example of a member page.

SlideShare membership is free, and members can comment on each other's presentations, which makes the site interactive. By allow-

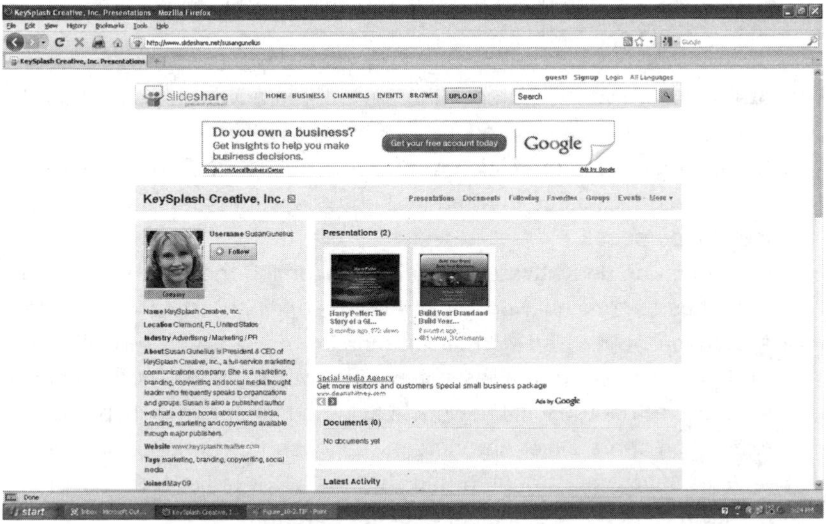

Figure 10.3   A SlideShare member page

ing people to comment on your presentations and share them through e-mail and embedding, you increase the exposure that your business and your presentations get, which can lead to indirect marketing success.

EzineArticles.com

EzineArticles.com (at www.ezinearticles.com) is a site for sharing the articles you write. Simply follow the editorial guidelines posted on the site, and submit your articles. Accepted articles are published on the site with a link to your own author page. Users can leave comments on articles they enjoy, making the site somewhat social. Furthermore, articles published on EzineArticles.com typically rank well in search engine results, so try to write with keywords in mind.

QUICK TIP

To ensure you don't violate any search engine optimization rules, always repurpose your online content rather than republishing it. In other words, take the time to modify your content for different sites where you plan to publish it, so each piece is unique.

Your articles should not be self-promotional. That means publishing articles on an article repository site such as EzineArticles.com is best for raising your own credibility and boosting brand awareness over the long term.

Content Sharing for Business Quick-Start Plan

Content sharing is an important part of your social media marketing efforts. Fortunately, the social Web provides tools that make it quick and easy to share content with a wide audience. Most of these sites offer free registration and use.

1. Join a photo-sharing site like Flickr, and upload images that add value to your target audience's online experience.
2. Connect with other Flickr users that you know or who would be interested in your content. Leave comments on their submissions, and add them to your friend network.
3. Search for Flickr groups where your target audience spends time, or create your own group for your target audience.
4. Create a SlideShare account, and upload your presentations.

5. Search for other interesting presentations, and leave comments to connect with other members. You can also share interesting presentations on your blog, your Twitter profile, and so on.
6. Consider writing and submitting articles on sites like EzineArticles.com and Squidoo.com, or write guest blog posts for other popular blogs related to your business. (Always reach out to the blog owner first, to ensure he or she accepts guest blog posts and to get any guest-blogging requirements before you begin writing your post.)
7. Leave comments on other articles you enjoy to get on the authors' radar screens.
8. Promote your photo-sharing, SlideShare, and other content-sharing profiles on your website, blog, social networking profiles, e-mails, and so on to increase your connections and further sharing of your content.

Chapter 11

Audio and Video

Billions of videos are viewed online each month on sites like YouTube, blip.tv, TubeMogul.com, Vimeo, and more (see Appendix B for a longer list). And the numbers continue to grow each month. Businesses can get some of that video traffic, too. You just have to create, upload, and promote your own interesting and useful videos. Creating videos is so easy these days with the use of a video camera, and uploading to a site like YouTube just takes a few minutes. You can even create your own branded video show page on YouTube and other video-sharing sites. The potential for brand building, word-of-mouth marketing, and direct and indirect selling is amazing.

While online video usually is best for indirect marketing, some businesses successfully walk a fine line between indirect and direct marketing by promoting products in entertaining ways in their videos. For example, to promote the Blendtec blender, Blendtec CEO Tom Dickinson stars in a series of videos on the Blendtec YouTube channel (www.youtube.com/user/blendtec) called "Will It Blend?" In each of these videos, he puts the Blendtec blender to the test. Tom blends anything from an iPhone to a pair of skis in an attempt to show just how great the Blendtec blender is. The Blendtec videos have become an Internet sensation. The Blendtec YouTube channel had just under 100 uploaded videos at the time this book was written, with just under 100 million views, and the channel had nearly a quarter million subscribers.

Before You Tackle Multimedia Publishing, Create a Strategy

Creating videos and audio content is a great way to engage people online by appealing to different senses than the written word can. Automatically, video and audio content creates a different consumer experience than written content does, and many consumers prefer visual or auditory stimuli to reading text. Take some time to search for videos related to your business or industry on a site like YouTube, and notice which types of videos are getting the most views and comments. Your goal should be to create content that adds a new dimension to your business but is interesting, useful, or entertaining enough to entice viewers to watch it, comment about it, and share it with their own audiences. Online video is usually very easy to embed in other websites and blogs, so make sure your audio and video content is published with permission settings that allow other people to republish and share it for maximum business exposure.

Once you know your goals for using audio and video to market your business, you can begin thinking about the kind of content you want to publish. You can either create highly professional audio and video (an excellent example is Shelly Palmer's YouTube channel, at www.youtube.com/user/Media30dotcom), or you can do it yourself, giving your content a more personal feeling. Remember the story about Gary Vaynerchuk from *Wine Library TV* (http://tv.winelibrary .com) told in Chapter 2? Gary's videos are not filmed in a professional studio, nor are they scripted, but Gary's personality and passion for his topic and business make him hard to resist. That's one of the reasons his videos are so popular. You need to decide how you want your business and brand portrayed through online audio and video and then create videos that match that image.

The content of your videos also needs to match your brand image. Many business owners don't know what to talk about in audio or video content, but who would have thought that videos by a guy who compares wine flavors to rocks (Gary Vaynerchuk) would become popular? The truth of the matter is that as long as your videos are interesting, useful, helpful, or entertaining, you're on the right track. For some ideas, see the sidebar "Audio and Video Content Suggestions." Publishing online video and audio shouldn't be done in an effort to catch lightning in a bottle and be the next viral marketing

AUDIO AND VIDEO CONTENT SUGGESTIONS

- Interview employees, customers, industry experts, and any other interesting person you can find that your target audience is likely to respond to.

- Share behind-the-scenes clips from your office.

- Show snippets from your office activity or party to prove your business is really human.

- Take videos of your employees helping at charity events.

- Publish videos taken at trade shows you attend. For example, talk to people on the trade show floor, or share snippets from roundtables or seminars. Be sure to get permission to record at and publish videos from events.

- Share tips or answer questions.

- Demonstrate how to use your products.

- Get outside and film yourself offering your expert opinion or insight.

rage. Videos that go viral are usually not business related. Instead, your online video and audio strategy should be a long-term strategy that focuses on brand and relationship building.

Tips for Creating Online Audio and Video

Once you have defined your strategy for online audio and video, you need to make sure you have the necessary equipment to create, edit, and upload your content. For highly professional audio and video, you might have to hire a video company to help you, but most small and midsize businesses that use online audio and video for social media marketing create their own videos with fairly simple equipment and editing. As long as your content is great and the quality of your video and audio is good, you don't have to hire a professional to record your content.

For example, you can use your own digital video camera to create your online video. Many people use an inexpensive Flip Video Camera to record videos, particularly when they're at conferences and trade shows. You can even use a webcam and a microphone hooked up to your computer (both are built into Macs). Decent-quality webcams and microphones aren't expensive. For editing your audio and video, you can use tools like iMovie or GarageBand (which come preinstalled on Macs) or Windows Movie Maker (which is compatible with Windows-based computers). You can also purchase fairly inexpensive audio- and video-editing software from well-known companies like Adobe and Corel. Remember, you're not trying to create an Academy Award–winning movie. You're just trying to create interesting content that matches your brand image.

Try to keep the running time of your online video content to less than five minutes. Research shows that after three to four minutes, the number of people watching a video drops significantly. Your most intriguing content should be shown early, so your most important messages aren't missed. It's also a good idea to create a consistent, professional introduction and closing for your audio and video content. That could include an image with text or music with a voiceover. Just remember to make sure you use images and music that carry copyright

QUICK TIP

You can find royalty-free music online at a site like RoyaltyFreeMusic .com (www.royaltyfreemusic.com), and you can find royalty-free images on sites like iStockphoto (www .istockphoto.com) or morgueFile (www.morguefile.com).

licenses allowing you to republish them. Also, make sure your closing includes your website URL and your contact information. The "Blogger in the Spotlight" interview series on the Newstex YouTube channel (www.youtube.com/user/newstex), shown in Figure 11.1, offers an excellent example of a simple but effective video introduction and closing.

Tools for Uploading and Sharing Video Content

Several online video-sharing sites are available, with YouTube being the most popular. While using YouTube to publish your online video content means it will reside on the most heavily trafficked online video site, it also means your content can get lost in the clutter of videos uploaded by teenagers professing their love for the hot new celebrity

Figure 11.1 The Newstex YouTube channel

of the moment. Smaller online video sites have fewer users but might offer a more targeted audience. The best-case scenario is to create a YouTube channel as your home base for your online video content and experiment with other online video sites to see if they deliver a better return in terms of views and further sharing of your videos. In this section, you can learn about the benefits of using YouTube and TubeMogul .com, two excellent options for uploading and sharing your online video content.

YouTube

YouTube (www.youtube.com) is owned by Google and gets the vast majority of all online video traffic. You can sign up for a YouTube account and create your own branded YouTube channel to publish your video content. You can include a description of your business and a link to your website on your channel page, which you can easily promote with your unique URL. You can also add descriptions and keyword tags to every video you upload to increase the number of people who find your videos through searches.

YouTube becomes social when people leave comments on videos and share them through social bookmarking, Twitter, and so on. Make sure viewers are allowed to embed your videos into their own websites and blogs to increase the virality of your content.

TubeMogul.com

TubeMogul.com (www.tubemogul.com) is one of the newer online video-publishing and -sharing sites, but it has grown quickly because with a single upload, your video can be distributed to a variety of other sites, including Google, Bing, Yahoo!, YouTube, blip.tv, Dailymotion, MySpace, and more. TubeMogul.com also offers excellent tracking and reporting features that can be helpful for analyzing what content works and what content needs improvement, so you can modify your online video strategy as needed.

You need to have accounts with each of the other sites where you want your videos distributed, and you're limited to a certain number of video uploads and deployments each month, depending on the type of account you have with TubeMogul.com (there are free and paid accounts). However, TubeMogul.com offers an easy way to get additional exposure for your video content with very little effort, so it's worth testing.

Tools for Uploading and Sharing Audio Content

Audio content can come in the form of individual audio files, podcasts, or online talk shows. Fortunately, a variety of free tools can help you upload and share your audio with a wider audience than simply uploading individual files to your blog or website would allow, and some of those sites make it very easy for you to further distribute your audio content to Apple's iTunes, putting it in front of an even bigger audience. Two of the most popular tools for publishing audio content are described in this section (you can find more in Appendix B).

BlogTalkRadio

BlogTalkRadio (at www.blogtalkradio.com) is a popular website for creating online talk shows. The site offers both free and paid accounts, as well as branded show pages and unique show URLs, which include links to the owner's website. You can create your own show and record it using your telephone. Guests can call in to participate on your live or prerecorded show. It's a flexible site with a strong community of people behind it. Members can also leave comments and join discussions on other shows, and since shows include buttons to make it easy to share them on social bookmarking sites, Twitter, and so on, people can also help spread your content beyond the BlogTalkRadio community. BlogTalkRadio also offers tools to help you easily integrate your show into Facebook, Twitter, iTunes, and more.

Blubrry

Blubrry (at www.blubrry.com) is a popular site for publishing podcasts. You can upload, publish, and host your podcast content on your own branded show page on Blubrry, which includes a description, a unique URL, and a link to your website. You can also easily integrate your podcast into iTunes, Twitter, and more. People can subscribe to your podcast, share it on social bookmarking and social networking sites, and embed it on their own blogs or websites, making it easy for your content to spread beyond the Blubrry site. Audience members can also leave comments on your show, so it becomes interactive. There is even a Blubrry WordPress plugin that makes it extremely easy to integrate your podcast into your blog.

Audio and Video for Business Quick-Start Plan

Getting started with online audio and video entails creating the necessary accounts and acquiring the equipment you need to produce content. Next, create your content and upload it to your accounts so you can share it with the world.

1. Create a YouTube account and a YouTube channel.
2. Search for people creating content that would interest your target audience, and leave comments on interesting videos. Share videos on social bookmarking sites, and embed videos in your blog posts to further the discussion and build relationships with other video publishers and your audience.
3. Create and upload your own video content to your YouTube channel. Be sure to write good descriptions of your videos and tag them with relevant keywords to increase search traffic.
4. Create a BlogTalkRadio account and your own show page.
5. Search for other shows your target audience would be interested in, and leave comments on those shows. Share links to those

shows on your social bookmarking accounts, Twitter, etc., and blog about them to build relationships with other people.

6. Record content for your own show.
7. Promote your audio and video content on your blog, website, social networking profiles, social bookmarking accounts, Twitter profile, and anywhere else you can think of to increase awareness and listeners.

Chapter 12

E-Books, Reviews, Webinars, and Other Social Media Marketing Opportunities

The tools of the social Web offer a wide variety of ways to promote your business, but there are more opportunities for building your business than just using the most common tools people think of when they hear the term *social media*. In other words, the conversations that happen on the social Web outside of blogs, social networking, and Twitter are also social media marketing opportunities that you can leverage to directly and indirectly market your business.

As you learned in Chapter 6, the most important components of social media marketing (the four Cs of social media marketing participation) are content creation, content sharing, connections, and community building—all of which lead to conversations and relationships. Don't be afraid to get creative in your use of social media marketing to build your business. This chapter introduces you to a number of individual social media marketing opportunities that can help to grow your online presence through content marketing, establish your reputation, and spread your brand message across the social Web.

Writing E-Books for Content Creation, Content Sharing, and Content Marketing

You can write an e-book about any subject that could be interesting or helpful to your customers or target audience in an effort to build your online presence and reputation through content creation and sharing. There are really no rules for writing an e-book, so if you enjoy writing, then an e-book can be a great opportunity for you to share your expertise and connect with a broader online audience.

If your e-book includes valuable content, then people are likely not just to read it but also to share it with other people by blogging about it, mentioning it on Twitter or on their Facebook or LinkedIn profiles, and so on. The most important thing to remember when you write an e-book is that it should not read like a promotional brochure or an extended advertisement. Instead, your e-book should offer valuable information that goes beyond your website or blog. For example, as described in "Newstex and 'The Truth About . . .' E-Book Series," a company called Newstex uses e-books as a tool to explain its primary business (content syndication) and to dispel misunderstandings related to the syndication industry.

NEWSTEX AND "THE TRUTH ABOUT . . ." E-BOOK SERIES

Newstex is a content aggregation and syndication company serving online publishers and content distributors. The syndication market is varied and confusing to content publishers, so instead of simply creating a brochure that says licensed syndication through Newstex is the best kind of syndication, the company chose to create a series of e-books (shown in Figure 12.1) that clearly explain the process of licensed content syndication and the differences between syndication methods. The series is titled "The Truth About . . . ," and each e-book explores a different aspect of content syndication.

Of course, the e-books make a case for why licensed syndication through Newstex can benefit content publishers and distributors, but they provide more valuable information than mere marketing messages. In addition, the e-books are freely accessible to anyone, and they are copyrighted using a Creative Commons Attribution license. The copyright page of each e-book encourages readers to freely share the e-books across the

Figure 12.1   "The Truth About . . ." e-book series from Newstex

Web, which has led to thousands of downloads of each e-book within very short time frames. Additional sharing has occurred on blogs, Twitter, social networking sites, and other social media.

If writing does not come easily to you, it's easy to hire a freelance writer to help. Simply place an ad on a freelance website like the ones listed in Chapter 7, asking for an e-book writer. Be sure to include the book length in number of words or pages and topic for the e-book in your ad, and request samples of the writer's previous work. Writers charge a wide variety of fees for writing e-books, typically based on the writer's experience, the length of the e-book, and any research required to write it, which can greatly affect the amount of time it takes for the writer to complete the project.

Formatting Your E-Book

There are a few things you can do to make it easy for people to view and read your e-book conveniently. First, consider formatting your e-book using a landscape layout (like a presentation), rather than in a portrait layout (like a word processing document or a traditional book). That's because many people read e-books online, and a landscape format fits their computer screens better than a portrait format does. Also, use a font that's easy to read online and offline, such as Verdana or Georgia, which are commonly used online for their readability, and use a typeface that is at least 14 points, because small font sizes are difficult to read online.

Your e-book should use colors that translate clearly both online and offline. A safe choice is to stick with a white background and bold colors for text and graphics. Typically, e-books are not long. Aim for approximately 20 pages in length to ensure you're offering enough information to make the e-book worthwhile but short enough that it's not intimidating or overwhelming. Finally, make sure your e-book is available for download in PDF format, and include a link to the free Adobe Reader software download page (http://get.adobe.com/reader), so people who don't already have the software on their computers can easily download it and access your e-book.

> **QUICK TIP**
>
> If you're writing e-books to grow your business over the long term, then you should not require registration or e-mail address submission for people to access your e-books. Furthermore, publish your e-books with a Creative Commons Attribution license, and offer them for free online. By allowing anyone to read your e-books and share them, you free your content to spread across the social Web, which helps to build your business significantly more than you can by obtaining some e-mail addresses or making a small amount of money from selling e-books.

Publishing Your E-Book

Save your e-book in PDF format, and upload it to your Web hosting account (described in Chapter 7). Then link to it everywhere you can think of. For example, add a page to your website that promotes your e-book, blog about it, tweet it, and mention it on your social networking profiles. You should also include a link to your e-book in your e-mail signature, in e-mail newsletters, in the sidebar on every page of your website or blog, and so on. You can even advertise your

> **QUICK TIP**
>
> Marketing expert and author David Meerman Scott's e-books offer an excellent example of good design. You can view his e-books at Scott's website, www.davidmeermanscott.com/products_ebooks.htm.

e-book online by placing ads on blogs, websites, Facebook, LinkedIn, and more.

To analyze downloads of your e-book, you can use a URL-shortening service like bit.ly (http://bit.ly) to create a unique URL for the page where your e-book is available, and use that URL everywhere you include a link to your e-book. That way, you can keep track of how many times your e-book is downloaded to help you gauge its success.

Using Webinars as a Social Media Marketing Tool

Do you have knowledge of your industry that other people can learn from? Do you know experts who can share information with your target customers that could be useful or helpful to them? If so, then you can hold online seminars, called *webinars*, to educate people about a wide variety of concepts related to your business. You can even offer your own services as a virtual speaker, so you can participate in other organizations' webinars to broaden your online exposure.

Using online event-planning tools and meeting tools, you can invite people to attend your webinars, accept responses and payment for attendance, and hold your webinars online with or without audience participation via phone or chat. For example, Skype allows you to hold free voice, chat, or video conference calls that might suit your needs. There are also tools that enable you to use a visual presentation during your webinar, and you and attendees can call into a predetermined phone number to participate. It's a very simple process, and there are both free and paid tools that can help you host your own webinars.

Hosting a Webinar

Choose a webinar topic that your target customer audience would find useful and valuable. Free webinars will get you the most exposure, so as long as you don't have to pay speakers to participate and your goal is to use webinars as a marketing tool, then you should try to offer them free of charge to participants.

You can invite people to your webinar using tools from a service like Eventbrite (www.eventbrite.com). Facebook, LinkedIn, and Twitter have event apps that make it very easy to promote your webinar and accept responses to your invitations.

To hold your webinar, you can use an online meeting tool such as the following:

- **GoToWebinar:** www.gotomeeting.com/fec/webinar
- **WebEx:** http://webex.com/how-it-works/for-online-events.html
- **Adobe Connect:** www.adobe.com/products/acrobatconnectpro/
- **Yugma (free online tool):** www.yugma.com

Promoting a Webinar

You can promote a webinar across your social Web profiles via your blog, Twitter stream, Facebook events, LinkedIn events, and so on.

Include a link to the sign-up page everywhere that you mention the webinar, and make sure you remind people more than once that the event is coming. Often, people put off registering for an event, thinking they'll have time to do it later, only to forget completely until it's too late. Reminders are important.

QUICK TIP

Choose an online meeting tool that meets your budget as well as your needs related to the number of attendees, participation methods, video streaming, recording the webinar, and so on.

You should also track where your webinar attendees heard about your event, so you can see which efforts are worth repeating or enhancing in order to maximize attendance at your next webinar. Some online event tools allow you to do this. You can also use a free or paid survey tool to send out a survey after the webinar to get feedback from attendees. Sites with survey tools include SurveyMonkey (www .surveymonkey.com) and SurveyGizmo (www.surveygizmo.com).

Afterward, make the webinar presentation available via your blog and SlideShare. (Be sure to link your SlideShare account to your social networking profiles, as discussed in Chapter 9.) Encourage attendees to share the presentation with their own audiences to increase your exposure from the webinar even after the event ends.

Online Reviews and Local Search as Social Media Marketing Tools

While writing e-books and hosting webinars might not be for everyone, getting online reviews about your business should be. That's because research consistently shows that people are influenced more by other people's opinions (even strangers online) when making buying decisions than by any other form of marketing or communications. Fortunately, there are a variety of ways to get people to publish online reviews about your business, which can be shared across the social Web.

Of course, you can always ask your social Web connections to write reviews about your business, products, and services, but don't limit yourself to your existing network. You can increase the potential for getting online reviews by making sure your business is listed in local search engines and business directories that include review features, and you can even pay for reviews.

Using Local Search and Business Directories for Search Engine Optimization and Reviews

Many online business directories, local search sites, and search engines offer businesses the opportunity to list their contact information. It's important that your business be listed on as many of these sites as possible to boost your online presence and increase the chances that people can find you in Web searches. However, many of these tools offer an additional feature: customer reviews. Positive online reviews can give your business a big boost, so ensuring consumers have the opportunity to write reviews across the Web is a great way to help your business.

Local directory reviews can drive awareness and traffic to any business. For example, Metamorphous Hair Salon, located in central Florida, was feeling the pinch from the 2009 recession and needed help finding new clients. When money is tight, one of the first luxuries women eliminate is hair-coloring and related services, choosing less expensive over-the-counter tools instead of professional salons. To combat the shift, Metamorphous's owner, Jill St. Peter, was open to new ideas to bring in new clients and decided to leverage the social Web to build her online reputation and get her name in front of consumers who were actively looking for the services she provides at her salon.

As is the case for most small businesses, Metamorphous did not have a huge marketing budget, and St. Peter realized that traditional advertising was not bringing in the results she needed. She learned about the free and low-cost alternatives available to her on the social Web, as well as how a social Web presence can help build relationships and boost search engine rankings. St. Peter opted to use Facebook

DON'T FORGET!

Of course, when people publish reviews online, there is a strong possibility that they'll publish negative reviews, too. Remember the story of Dell told in Chapter 3. Don't try to control the online conversation by suppressing negative comments. Instead, evaluate the source, and decide whether you want to ignore it, respond to it in an effort to nudge the conversation in a more positive direction, or bury it with amazing content. You can read more about negative online publicity in Chapter 5.

and local search tools to get her name in front of more people. She made sure her business was represented on sites like CitySearch and Google Local Business Center (now Google Places), and she asked some of her customers to write reviews on those sites. Once the first review was published, other customers stepped forward of their own accord and added their reviews. Within two months, St. Peter's clientele increased by 10 percent.

Following is a list of popular websites for local business searches and business directories. Many of these sites offer the option for visitors to publish reviews of businesses found on the sites. Conduct searches on each site, and modify your existing listings to ensure they're accurate, or add your business listing if it's not already included.

- **CitySearch:** www.citysearch.com
- **Yahoo! Local:** http://listings.local.yahoo.com
- **Google Places:** http://google.com/places
- **Yellow Pages:** www.yellowpages.com
- **Yelp:** www.yelp.com
- **Kudzu:** www.kudzu.com
- **DexKnows:** www.dexknows.com

Paying for Online Reviews and Comments

A variety of websites allow businesses to pay online publishers to write about their products and services. Sometimes, businesses send products directly to influential or targeted bloggers to test and review, or they might publish a review opportunity on a site that matches advertisers with online publishers. Any way you slice it, paying for online reviews or comments is dangerous territory, because the Federal Trade Commission (FTC) issues regulations related to paid endorsements, which have fairly strict requirements that many businesses and publishers don't follow. The FTC updates regulations annually, so it's important to know what the current laws are before you pay for online reviews or endorsements. Remember, ignorance is not a valid defense in a court of law, so it's essential that you review and follow the rules defined by the government and any review sites you use to ensure you're doing everything that you're supposed to be doing.

It's also important ethically that reviewers disclose any compensation they received for writing a review and provide an honest, accurate review of their actual experiences with the item or business being reviewed. Whether you approach a blogger or other online publisher directly and request a review in return for a product sample or monetary compensation or you access reviewers through a third-party website that matches advertisers with publishers, you should make sure that reviews published about your business are legally and ethically appropriate.

QUICK TIP

You can access the regulations related to online reviews and endorsements in Title 16, Part 255 of the Code of Federal Regulations (16 CFR 255) on the FTC website: http://ecfr.gpoaccess.gov/cgi/t/ text/text-idx?c=ecfr&sid=ebedd671 1cc1541edb55aceb9a1638f3&rgn= div5&view=text&node=16 :1.0.1.2.22&idno=16.

Many businesses reach out to bloggers and online publishers directly via e-mail to request reviews, and some post paid review and comment opportunities on freelance websites like the ones mentioned in Chapter 7 or on craigslist. Here are a few of the most popular websites that connect publishers with advertisers for sponsored reviews and comments:

- **SocialSpark:** http://socialspark.com
- **PayPerPost:** https://payperpost.com
- **Sponsored Tweets:** http://sponsoredtweets.com

Be certain to read all of the rules and requirements published on any sponsored review sites on which you publish opportunities, to ensure you're always in compliance. When in doubt, err on the side of caution. You don't want to be caught paying for a review without disclosing it, because that can cause more harm than good. For an example of how paying for online reviews can backfire, see "Belkin Gets Caught Paying for Positive Reviews Online."

BELKIN GETS CAUGHT PAYING FOR POSITIVE REVIEWS ONLINE

In January 2009, computer and electronics accessory maker Belkin was caught soliciting positive reviews for its products on sites like Amazon .com, Buy.com, and Newegg.com when *The Daily Background* published a screen shot of a paid review opportunity that Belkin published on Amazon's Mechanical Turk site (a service that matches workers with tasks to complete for payment). The opportunity made it clear that workers were expected to give the product being reviewed a rating of 5 out of 5 (or 100 percent), the highest rating possible, regardless of whether or not they had ever used or owned the product. In fact, the opportunity required workers to pretend they did use or own the product in order to receive payment. The opportunity also required workers to mark other negative reviews as unhelpful. Payment for completing the task was reported as $0.65 per positive review.

Shortly after the story broke on *The Daily Background*, Belkin released an apology letter, which is still available in the Belkin online press room (http://www.belkin.com/pressroom/letter.html). In the letter, Belkin's president, Mark Reynoso, apologized for the incident related to Mechanical Turk and stated it was an isolated incident. Unfortunately for Belkin, the problem didn't end there.

Next, a Belkin employee spoke to one of the most popular blogs, Gizmodo.com, and claimed that Belkin had been soliciting and paying for positive consumer reviews for a very long time. As you would expect, *Gizmodo* published the Belkin employee's claims, and when that story broke, Belkin's apology letter failed to re-create the intended trust.

Your goal in getting reviewers to write about your business online is to find people who can publish honest reviews on sites where your target audience spends time. Think of it this way: a review about a Hummer would be a waste of money on a blog about saving the environment. Placing reviews works just like placing ads. You need to find sites that already have an audience of potential customers who would be interested in trying your products and services or talking about them with other people by spreading the word across the social Web.

For example, a review published on a highly focused niche blog is likely to be shared among a smaller, highly interested audience.

A review published on a popular blog is likely to be linked to from other blogs, rank high in search engine searches, get tweeted about, be linked to on social networking sites, and get shared on social bookmarking sites, giving it wide exposure across a broad, less focused audience. That's the type of word-of-mouth marketing that only social media can deliver!

PART III

Dive In for 30 Minutes a Day

The How of Social Media Marketing

Chapter 13

Indirect Marketing

In simplest terms, indirect marketing is any form of marketing that is not primarily intended to solicit an immediate (or direct) purchase. Social media marketing is an effective long-term indirect marketing strategy that can be supplemented with compelling short-term direct marketing tactics. In other words, a Twitter profile is an excellent tool for brand building (indirect marketing), which can also be used to generate sales (direct marketing).

The best social media marketing plans include both indirect and direct marketing strategies and tactics, but your primary focus should always be the long-term indirect marketing opportunities of brand building, relationship building, and business building. Short-term sales spikes are wonderful, but by definition they are often short-lived. Conversely, a long-term social media marketing strategy can benefit a business for years to come.

Using Social Media Marketing for Research, Segmentation, and Targeting

Throughout this book, you've learned how the tools of the social Web can help you gain valuable insight about your customers and your competitors, which is another form of indirect marketing, because with knowledge comes the ability to recognize and exploit opportuni-

153

ties. Many marketers refer to the social Web as the "always-on focus group," meaning if you listen to the conversations happening across the social Web, you can collect a significant amount of qualitative research data about your industry, products, customers, and competitors. In recent years, people have used Twitter conversations as a tool to track the success of newly released movies, political elections, and more—often with great accuracy. The information you need to understand in order to grow your business is out there on the social Web; you just need to do some legwork to find it and then listen to it.

Once you collect the research information you need to begin creating strategies and tactics, you can identify your target audience and find those people on the social Web. You need to start spending time where your target audience is already hanging out in order to develop relationships with those people so you can entice them to visit you on your branded online destinations, where you can further those relationships and offer more amazing content and conversations. That is how you develop a band of brand advocates who will talk about your brand and business to their own audiences across the social Web, giving you the most valuable form of word-of-mouth marketing with little monetary investment.

As with all aspects of your business, not all of your customers are the same, and you need to understand the diverse segments of like consumers within your overall audience. Your audience can be segmented demographically (by age, education, gender, income, etc.), as is traditionally done by marketers, but the social Web also offers an invaluable opportunity to segment your audience behaviorally. Not only do online behaviors affect where people spend time online, but those behaviors also affect what people do online. For example, some people love Twitter, while others would never read a tweet. Those people could all be part of the same demographic profile, but their online activities place them in very different behavioral segments of your audience.

Relying on demographic segmentation alone when building your social media marketing strategy will lead to failure, or at the very least, you won't reach full potential. Fortunately, the Web analytics tools discussed in Chapter 21 can help you track where people travel within your website or blog, what keywords they use to find your site in searches, and so on, but much of your behavioral analysis has to be done by communicating, listening, and participating on the social Web. In other words, use your relationships with your audience to understand what they want and need from you, *and* spend time digesting as much information as you can across the social Web conversation to better understand the online behaviors of people who match the various segments of your target audience's behavioral profiles. Not only can understanding the behaviors of your best customers help you to better deliver more of the content they want and need, but it can also help you find more people like them. It's a win-win situation for any business.

Why Indirect Marketing Is an Important Part of Social Media Marketing

Indirect marketing helps spread the word about your brand and business and raises brand awareness and recognition. The more people hear about your brand and talk about it (word-of-mouth marketing), the more opportunities there are for people to seek out your brand or business and make a purchase. In time, trust develops, and people will become loyal to your brand. Once they're loyal, they'll advocate your brand and protect it against negativity. A band of brand advocates is a powerful online force that can make or break a business.

For example, Lorrie Thomas of Web Marketing Therapy (www .webmarketingtherapy.com) successfully built her business through indirect marketing on the social Web. Web Marketing Therapy uses its business blog as the nucleus of its social media marketing activities, which also include a show on BlogTalkRadio and three Twitter accounts. As Lorrie explains, "Social media marketing is about relationships and having conversation that offers compounding interest: the more tentacles you have out there, the more people find you. We use social media marketing to build awareness and help customers. I always say, 'We use social media to serve, not to sell.'"

For Lorrie Thomas and Web Marketing Therapy, social media have helped the company grow beyond its California roots to a wider geographic reach, new business ventures, speaking engagements, and more. Lorrie points out that to be successful in social media, you need to use your own voice and have fun through collaboration and conversations. According to Lorrie, "Our agency would not be what it is today without social media marketing. We wouldn't have the reputation we have. Social media has positioned us in the market, and now, 75 percent of our business is completely social media codependent."

It's important to remember as you're building your social media marketing strategy that nearly every activity you do on the social Web could be considered a form of indirect marketing. All four Cs of social media marketing participation introduced in Chapter 6 (content creation, content sharing, connections, and community building) can be used for indirect marketing. For example, you can create content on your blog, share content through social bookmarking, build communities in a LinkedIn group, and make connections on Facebook. The opportunities for indirect marketing on the social Web are virtually limitless. To see how a small video game company used social media marketing to build its business to a global success, read "The Social Media Marketing Success of Golden Tee Golf."

QUICK TIP

When you find a positive review of your business or products, share it on Twitter, Facebook, your business blog, and so on. Teusner Wines does this very successfully through its @teusnerwine Twitter profile. In fact, Teusner Wines often tweets a positive review of its wines a few times in a single day to ensure a broad audience sees it.

THE SOCIAL MEDIA MARKETING SUCCESS OF GOLDEN TEE GOLF

Golden Tee Golf (www.goldentee.com) is a 120-employee company that uses social media to build its business on two levels: embedded into its video games and in daily social media participation. Golden Tee Golf is a social game that can be played with friends and over a live network. To keep the game relevant to a new generation of players, Daniel Schrementi, director of new media for Incredible Technologies (the maker of Golden Tee Golf), explains: "Social media marketing allows us to add value to both customers and our company. You don't see a lot of companies who add value to both customers and the company. The Golden Tee Golf social media activities add value to players by giving them something that they want, and it adds marketing value to the company through brand impressions and word-of-mouth."

Golden Tee Golf uses YouTube, which is seamlessly integrated into the game, to allow players to share videos in the "Great Shot Replay." When players hit a hole in one, a screen opens where they can upload the video replay to YouTube and share it with their friends. Within one year of the

Figure 13.1 The Golden Tee Golf YouTube channel

YouTube feature's debut, 100,000 videos were uploaded and received over 1 million views. The feature also generated a significant amount of press.

Additionally, Golden Tee Golf is active on Facebook, where the company offers discounts and coupons as well as a feature that allows other Facebook users to add a status to their profiles saying, "I'm playing now at [name of the location where they're playing Golden Tee Golf at any given moment]." Golden Tee Golf also uses Twitter to communicate with customers and sponsors a weekly contest with Twitter users that uses the hashtag #GTThursday, so people can easily follow the conversation.

According to Schrementi, "Customers were hard to reach before social media. Die-hard Golden Tee Golf players were vocal, but casual players didn't come to our website. However, they do friend us on Facebook, and they do communicate with us when we use social media tools to answer questions and start conversations." Golden Tee Golf also leverages tools like TweetDeck and Google Alerts to keep on top of conversations related to specific keywords. "We reach out to people when they talk about us to help or just with a fun message. It makes people know we care," Schrementi says.

Golden Tee Golf offers a variety of useful features on its website, but the company didn't see a lot of Web visitors until its business blog (http://blog.goldentee.com) was mentioned on a popular gaming blog. Suddenly, tens of thousands of people began visiting the Golden Tee Golf blog each day, and the company realized that its blog offered significant potential in attracting a different audience than its YouTube videos or website typically attracted.

Schrementi points out, "It's really hard to quantify our success directly from social media marketing, but since we started last year, our online presence and hits to our website have doubled. That growth can be tied directly to links from social media sites like Facebook, YouTube, and Twitter. For example, the number of videos on the Golden Tee Golf Channel on YouTube grew from a few to 100,000." (The channel is shown in Figure 13.1, on the previous page.) Schrementi continues, "It's easy to drive more traffic by using the free tools on the social Web. This stuff is already on; you just join in. Our goal for Golden Tee Golf is more quality conversations."

Sample 30-Minute Social Media Marketing Plans for Indirect Marketing

Following are two simple 30-minute social media marketing plans that you can easily use or modify for your own business in order to indirectly market your business on the social Web. You can also find a blank Social Media Marketing Plan Worksheet in Appendix C, which you can use to create your own schedule for social media activities.

Indirect Marketing Sample Plan A

METHOD OF PARTICIPATION	TIME	ACTIVITY
Content creation	15 minutes	Write a blog post that is useful and interesting for your target audience. (For additional content sharing, link to other related articles or blog posts that inspired your post, or offer additional information or commentary.)
Content sharing	5 minutes	Read updates from the people you follow on Twitter, and retweet interesting tweets.

METHOD OF PARTICIPATION	TIME	ACTIVITY
Connections	5 minutes	Use Facebook social plugins to enhance connectivity and interactivity between your website and blog. Start by adding the Facebook Like button to your website and blog.
Community building	5 minutes	Respond to comments on your blog and direct messages sent to you on Twitter.

Indirect Marketing Sample Plan B

METHOD OF PARTICIPATION	TIME	ACTIVITY
Content creation	10 minutes	Write useful, interesting comments on other blog posts related to your business where your target audience or influencers spend time.
Content sharing	5 minutes	Tweet links to interesting blog posts you read.
Connections	10 minutes	Find your most active Twitter followers who tweet content related to your business, and look through their followers to find new, interesting people to follow.
Community building	5 minutes	Join conversations in a LinkedIn group related to your business.

Chapter 14

Brand Building

A brand is a promise to consumers that sets consumer expectations and meets those expectations in every customer interaction and experience. Building a brand involves three primary keys to success:

1. Consistency
2. Persistence
3. Restraint

Specifically, you need to continually communicate consistent messages and images related to your brand and know when an opportunity to extend your brand is not a good match.

Social media marketing presents an incredible opportunity to communicate your brand messages to a wide audience of people who will eventually help you spread those messages even further. In other words, you can build brand awareness, recognition, and loyalty through social media marketing, which organically supports what I call the four fundamental steps to brand-building success:

1. **Awareness:** People first hear of your brand or business.
2. **Recognition:** People hear your brand or business name and recall having heard of it previously.

3. **Memory:** People hear your brand or business name and remember what you do.
4. **Spreading the word:** People know your brand or business name well enough to talk to other people about it. They may have just heard of it and have a genuine interest in doing business with you, or they may have actually done business with you already.

To remember these four steps, think of the acronym ARMS, spelled with the first letter of each step.

Most of the brand building you can do for your business on the social Web is done indirectly, simply through your participation in online conversations. Every time you create content, share content, join a conversation, or make a new connection, you're getting your brand name in front of people and creating an opportunity for a customer to either recognize your brand again or learn about it for the first time. Brand building is a long-term marketing strategy, as social media marketing is a long-term strategy, so it's not surprising that they coexist so well. In fact, it could be argued that all social media marketing is a form of brand building. For example, check out the suggestions in "50 Social Media Marketing Activities to Build a Brand" to see how many activities you can participate in on the social Web that can directly or indirectly raise awareness, recognition, and loyalty of your brand.

Why Brand Building Is an Important Part of Social Media Marketing

A brand is a valuable intangible business asset. While "brand" doesn't appear on a company balance sheet, it can help boost a business to great success. For example, a brand like Harry Potter evokes emotions and loyalty that surpass anyone's original expectations for a children's book about a boy wizard. No matter what business you're in, making an effort to build a brand reputation and a brand promise that evokes emotions and establishes customer expectations for it should be a business imperative. If a children's fantasy book can become a global brand phenomenon thanks to the social Web, then your business can certainly reach your goals through social media marketing.

50 SOCIAL MEDIA MARKETING
ACTIVITIES TO BUILD A BRAND

1. Write a post on your business blog.
2. Comment on other blogs related to your business.
3. Feed your blog posts to your Twitter profile.
4. Publish multimedia tweets, including images and video using Twitpic or yfrog.
5. Post @reply tweets on Twitter.
6. Share images on Flickr.
7. Create a video, and upload it to YouTube.
8. Join a forum related to your business, and publish posts to that forum.
9. Feed your Twitter stream and your blog to your Facebook profile.
10. Feed your Twitter stream and your blog to your LinkedIn profile.
11. Answer questions on LinkedIn.
12. Make recommendations on LinkedIn.
13. Bookmark amazing content on sites like Digg and StumbleUpon.
14. Participate in a tweet chat.
15. Live-tweet an event.
16. Host a webinar.
17. Write an e-book.
18. Host an online talk show on BlogTalkRadio.
19. Create a Facebook page for your business.
20. In the sidebar of your blog, include a link inviting people to subscribe to your blog.
21. Set Google and Twitter alerts for your business name and keywords related to your business, and then join conversations as they happen.
22. Send direct messages to people who follow you on Twitter to strengthen your conversations and relationships with them.
23. Publish polls on your blog to get feedback and conduct research about your customers.
24. Record a podcast, and make it available for download on iTunes.
25. Publish weekly roundup posts on your blog where you link to great posts related to your business published across the blogosphere during the previous seven days. (These are also called *link love posts*.)
26. Create a Facebook group related to your business.
27. Create a LinkedIn group related to your business.
28. Search for groups related to your business on Facebook, and join them. (Be sure to participate.)

29. Join groups related to your business on LinkedIn, and actively participate. Be sure to feed your blog updates into the news feature in groups that allow it.
30. Publish content on article-sharing sites like EzineArticles.com.
31. Leave comments on online videos that you enjoy and are related to your business.
32. Write guest posts for other blogs related to your business.
33. Publish comments on your friends' Facebook walls and photos.
34. Invite other people to write guest posts on your blog to further share their content.
35. Start your own social network on Ning.
36. Use Twitter apps like Nearby Tweets and Localtweeps to find Twitter users in your area, and follow them to start a relationship.
37. Post local events to Twitter using Localtweeps or Twtvite.
38. Share coupons with your Twitter followers, using twtQpon.
39. Create your listing on Twitter directories like Twellow and ExecTweets.
40. Create your listing on local search sites like Yelp and Google Places.
41. Send samples to bloggers, and ask them to write review posts about your products.
42. Publish videos to your Facebook profile and page.
43. Upload your presentations to SlideShare.
44. Publicize your events on Facebook and LinkedIn, using Eventbrite.
45. Create a MySpace page for your business.
46. Join Google groups related to your business, and be active.
47. Use buttons and widgets to cross-promote your social profiles. For example, include button links to your Twitter, Facebook, and LinkedIn profiles in your blog's sidebar.
48. Comment on links that other people share on social bookmarking sites like Digg and StumbleUpon.
49. Upload your video content to TubeMogul.com, and make sure it's distributed to as many other video sites through TubeMogul.com as possible.
50. Participate in shows on BlogTalkRadio by calling in with questions and publishing comments.

Remember, brands are built not by companies but by the consumers who create those brands through experiences and emotions. Therefore, it's essential that you allow people to take control of the online conversation and experience your brand in their own ways. You can always nudge the online conversation in the right direction or correct inaccuracies, as discussed in Chapter 5, but allowing the conversation to flow at the hands of consumers is the most powerful form of word-of-mouth marketing and brand building that exists.

QUICK TIP

Provide opportunities across the social Web where people can share and experience your brand in the ways they choose.

Much of business growth these days comes from customer acquisition, recommendations, and recognition (meaning people remember a business and what it stands for). Since most people find information through a Google search or a trip across the Web, your business needs to be represented online. Your content needs to be search-friendly, easily accessible, and "shareworthy" (meaning people want to share it with their own audiences).

With that in mind, your online presence should be defined around a single identity. That might be your business name, product name, or even your personal name. No matter what name you choose to build your online presence around, be consistent. That name will become a tangible representation of your online brand. It will also be vital to your efforts at search engine optimization and search engine reputation management. To learn how one small business has successfully used the tools of the social Web to build awareness of her business and entire industry, see "Sharon Jakubecy Builds a Business from Scratch Through Social Media."

SHARON JAKUBECY BUILDS A BUSINESS FROM SCRATCH THROUGH SOCIAL MEDIA

Sharon Jakubecy teaches the Alexander Technique in Los Angeles to a varied clientele. Unfortunately, many people haven't heard of the Alexander Technique and its benefits for relieving pain and managing stress. But with the tools of the social Web readily available to her, Jakubecy is working to change that. In fact, she has built her entire business from scratch through a blog, Facebook, Twitter, and an online video where she demonstrates the Alexander Technique (see Figure 14.1).

Today, the Alexander Technique community of practitioners is putting a lot of joint effort into using Twitter and a Google Group to build aware-

Figure 14.1   Sharon Jakubecy's popular video demonstration of the Alexander Technique helped to build her business.

ness. For example, members of this community actively retweet each other's content in an effort to boost their presence online, and they share lessons, articles, testimonials, and more through their Google Group. Jakubecy explains, "I've gotten the most actual business from Facebook—mostly from networking with friends who saw my posts or YouTube video and reached out to me, telling me they needed my help. Word got around. Within one year of being on Twitter and about one and a half years on Facebook, I'm the busiest I've ever been. A couple of years ago, I needed a second job. My next goal is to start a real blog, especially a video blog."

Jakubecy sees her social media participation as a long-term marketing strategy. "I don't see it as I'm going to post a link and get customers," she says. "The members of the Alexander Community support each other in raising awareness of the Alexander Technique instead of competing. We're trying to get the technique into the public consciousness, and eventually, it will flow from people's mouths like yoga does now."

Jakubecy's social media efforts are supplemented by a lot of in-person networking at events. She has also placed some local print ads but is quick to point out that she gets "more from social media than print ads in terms of building my business." Her tip to other business owners is to take the time to "friend as many people as possible and get the word out so people know about you."

Sample 30-Minute Social Media Marketing Plans for Brand Building

As you develop your schedules for social media participation, refer to the following two sample social media marketing plans for brand building. Use the blank Social Media Marketing Plan Worksheet in Appendix C to create your own schedule.

Brand Building Sample Plan A

METHOD OF PARTICIPATION	TIME	ACTIVITY
Content creation	15 minutes	Create a podcast episode that teaches your audience something or shares valuable, useful information.
Content sharing	5 minutes	Find and bookmark great posts related to your business on social bookmarking sites like Digg and StumbleUpon.
Connections	5 minutes	Invite people to join your business's Facebook page.
Community building	5 minutes	Create a group on Facebook or LinkedIn, and publish interesting content that sparks conversations. (Be sure to promote your groups and invite people to join them.)

Brand Building Sample Plan B

METHOD OF PARTICIPATION	TIME	ACTIVITY
Content creation	15 minutes	Publish shareworthy blog posts that offer tips, help, or expert opinions.
Content sharing	5 minutes	Upload pictures to Flickr from your business events, inside your office, charity events, or other moments that personalize your business. Share them on Twitter and through your social networking profiles.

(continued)

Brand Building Sample Plan B *(continued)*

METHOD OF PARTICIPATION	TIME	ACTIVITY
Connections	5 minutes	Search for your competitors' friends on Facebook, and send friend requests to the people you want to connect with.
Community building	5 minutes	Add Facebook pages related to your business to your list of Likes, and join the conversation.

Chapter 15

Building Relationships and Communities

The social Web is, by definition, a social place. Instead of socializing in person, people can use the easily accessible technology of the 21st century to socialize with others from around the world in the comfort of their own homes and at any time of the day or night. A business owner who wants to build his or her business would be crazy not to participate. Instead of relying on local events, conferences, and trade shows to network with existing and potential customers, you can log onto Facebook and connect with and communicate with more people than you'd ever have time to meet at a trade show.

Think of it this way: every time you leave a comment on a blog, retweet someone's tweet or content, share a blog post through Digg, or update your LinkedIn status, you're starting or joining a conversation. The more interesting and valuable your content and conversations are, the more people will want to socialize with you. First, you need to introduce yourself and show them that you're interesting and that it's worthwhile for them to take time out of their busy days to listen to what you have to say. At an in-person event, this would happen with a handshake and a conversation, but on the social Web, it happens with a connection request, a comment, a retweet, and so on, followed by conversation and sharing. In other words, building relationships and communities on the social Web follows the same basic process as building relationships and communities in person. The difference is the tools you use to start and grow those relationships and communities.

Why Building Relationships and Communities Is an Important Part of Social Media Marketing

In the previous chapter, you were reminded of the importance of building a band of brand advocates who willingly talk about your business and brand and protect them from naysayers. Your band of brand advocates will be stronger and bigger if you make an effort to build relationships with the people who support and talk about your brand. For example, you might like your iPhone, but if Apple reached out to you personally to socialize with you and build a relationship with you with interesting and valuable conversation, you'd probably move from being just a fan to being a vocal advocate of all things Apple.

In other words, recognizing people and showing them that you value their opinions and experiences with your brand can add a level of emotional involvement that ties a person to a brand or business irrevocably. For example, loyal and vocal Harry Potter fans are often labeled as Harry Potter evangelists because they are so emotionally connected to the brand. Building relationships and communities on the social Web is practically a guaranteed way of deepening brand loyalty, brand advocacy, brand guardianship, and word-of-mouth marketing. To learn some of the most important things you need to do as an active participant on the social Web, see the sidebar "10 Tips to Build Relationships and Communities on the Social Web."

Liz Isaacs of Lotus Writing and Communications (www.lotuswritingcommunications.net) provides an excellent example of an entrepreneur leveraging the tools of the social Web to build relationships in order to grow a business. As Isaacs says, "Anyone who thinks they don't need social media, saying they don't have time or don't know how, is old school and wrong. As long as I'm on Twitter, LinkedIn, and Facebook, that's all I need to do, but I need to know my target market first and provide the right mix to meet their needs."

Isaacs uses social media marketing tools to share links she believes might be helpful to her audience and to help other people. For example, she retweets a lot of content published by others on Twitter to

10 TIPS TO BUILD RELATIONSHIPS AND COMMUNITIES ON THE SOCIAL WEB

1. Be active.
2. Acknowledge other people.
3. Be personable and accessible.
4. Be yourself.
5. Be honest.
6. Don't just talk about yourself.
7. Listen to what others have to say.
8. Continually seek out new relationships.
9. Don't try to control the conversation.
10. Understand who your connections are, and adjust your conversations to match different segments of your audience without compromising the consistency of your brand message.

recognize and acknowledge them. In addition to social networking, she also uses social bookmarking tools to share content. She does very little self-promotion, believing strongly that success in social media marketing comes from building relationships. Isaacs took the time to find where the people she needs to network with spend time online, and then she focused on getting involved in those same places. She explains: "The fact that I can connect with anyone in the world is amazing. Who has the budget to fly all over the country? Social media helps me reach people I wouldn't reach in normal circumstances. Even if you own a local business, social media helps you stay in contact with people locally, *and* it helps you grow outside of your local area."

Isaacs uses social media tools like Twitter apps to save time and work "smarter, not harder." She shares her social media marketing motto: "Work smart, be heard and be remembered." She reports, "My business has grown exponentially since I started using social media like LinkedIn and Twitter. It has been very beneficial to me."

While some social media tools make it very easy to build your own online community, you can also build relationships through any type of connection or conversation. For example,

QUICK TIP

Social media networking should not replace picking up the phone to call someone or meeting a person face-to-face. Instead, it should enhance and expand your traditional relationship-building efforts.

you don't have to belong to the same local business group to build relationships with other business owners in your community, just as you don't need to belong to the same Facebook group to build relationships with other people on the social Web. Social networking tools like LinkedIn, Facebook, and Ning allow people to create niche online destinations where people with similar interests can meet, but you shouldn't limit your online networking to established destinations. You can network through a comment on an online video, a retweeted link, a bookmarked page, or any other effort that connects you in some way (even indirectly) to other people. To learn how a local dentist used the tools of the social Web to build relationships and his dental practice, see "A New York City Dentist Leverages Social Media Marketing to Build Relationships and His Practice."

A NEW YORK CITY DENTIST LEVERAGES SOCIAL MEDIA MARKETING TO BUILD RELATIONSHIPS AND HIS PRACTICE

Dr. Michael Sinkin is a dentist whose office is located in a busy part of Midtown Manhattan. Knowing that most people find doctors and dentists through word-of-mouth marketing, Sinkin realized that the social Web offers a place to *talk* with people and jump-start word-of-mouth marketing. He hired Be Visible Associates to help him launch a new website reflecting the personality of his practice. Sinkin spends all of his time with his patients, leaving him very little time for anything else, so he was originally concerned that diving into social media marketing would be too much for him. However, he is very relationship-oriented, so by working with Be Visible Associates, he was able to create a plan that allowed him to tackle social media marketing in a less overwhelming manner.

Sinkin started a blog at http://michaelsinkindds.com/blog/ (see Figure 15.1), where he shares behind-the-scenes stories and "banter in the chair." He commutes to work via train each day and bought a laptop so he could write blog posts on his way home each night as a reflection on his day. His posts are easy for him to write, and the process has become fun and cathartic for him. He doesn't update his blog every day, but writes when something inspires him.

Soon Sinkin joined Twitter and Facebook. He linked his blog feed to his Twitter and Facebook accounts, and within two weeks of starting his Twitter profile, he acquired three new patients directly from Twitter. He uses tools like Monitter to find people in his area who are talking about topics related

Figure 15.1 Dr. Michael Sinkin's blog includes prominent links to his other social media profiles.

to his business, and he reaches out to them. Two of his early new customers that came to him through Twitter were tweeting about toothaches when he found their conversations through Monitter and reached out to them—not trying to sell his services, but rather offering information and tips to help them through their situations. As Sinkin explains, "You need to use a different language, not selling."

Sinkin views himself as a traditionalist in a new world. He sees social media as an extension of his personality that allows him to connect with interesting people. "We're very careful not to sell. It's about engagement and showing people, 'We can help you, and we're nice,'" he says. "When someone tweets about me and says I'm a great dentist with my user name, @sinkinfeeling, you can't buy that kind of publicity and word-of-mouth. Social media is a platform that allows me to reach a larger audience, but the people we're reaching are more targeted. I was prepared for it to take a while for me to see benefits from social media, but it happened faster than I expected. When I first started, I wasn't even looking at my e-mail every day, and now I feel like I'm on the cutting edge. I write one or two blog posts per week on the train, and I log into Facebook and Twitter one or two times per day. There is a learning curve to social media marketing, but once you learn how, it's fun."

Sample 30-Minute Social Media Marketing Plans for Building Relationships and Communities

You can develop your own plans for social media participation using the sample 30-minute social media marketing plans that follow, as well as the Social Media Marketing Plan Worksheet in Appendix C.

Building Relationships and Communities Sample Plan A

METHOD OF PARTICIPATION	TIME	ACTIVITY
Content creation	10 minutes	Start and respond to conversations on Twitter with @replies. Respond to comments left on your blog, and join in the conversation on other blogs by commenting on posts.
Content sharing	5 minutes	Retweet interesting tweets, and be sure to add your own opinion or commentary to the tweet.
Connections	5 minutes	Search for people in your target audience, and send friend and connection requests on Facebook and LinkedIn. Also, find more people to follow on Twitter.
Community building	10 minutes	Leave comments on other people's updates on their Facebook walls and LinkedIn profiles. Participate in Facebook, LinkedIn, and other group conversations.

Building Relationships and Communities Sample Plan B

METHOD OF PARTICIPATION	TIME	ACTIVITY
Content creation	10 minutes	Join conversations on forums related to your business.
Content sharing	5 minutes	Publish links on Twitter to content written by people you want to get to know. Be sure to include their Twitter @usernames in your tweets, so they know you tweeted their content.
Connections	5 minutes	Search for other people who share content related to your business on Digg, and friend them. Publish comments on their submissions that you like, and Digg them, too.
Community building	10 minutes	Plan a tweet chat related to your business, and promote it on Localtweeps and through your own tweets, social networking profiles, and blog. Be sure to create a hashtag specifically for the tweet chat, and include it in your promotional updates.

Chapter 16

Word-of-Mouth Marketing

Word-of-mouth marketing is one of the most powerful forms of marketing, and the social Web presents a perfect medium for conversation and word-of-mouth marketing to spread far and wide. Generating an online buzz about your business or brand can have a significant effect on your bottom line. People love to talk, so it stands to reason that if you give them something worthwhile to talk about, they'll discuss it. Consumers trust the referrals, recommendations, and opinions of other consumers more than they trust business communications. Whether a business sends messages through an ad, a letter, or a website, consumers are still more likely to trust a complete stranger's opinion about a business than they are to trust a business's marketing messages. Therefore, it makes perfect sense that the conversations that happen across the social Web can make or break a business if the online buzz about that business gets loud enough.

For businesses to effectively leverage social media tools to generate an online conversation related to their brands, products, and services, they need to get involved. People won't talk about you if they don't know who you are or why they should care about you. By building your brand and building relationships online, as you learned in Chapters 14 and 15, you boost the opportunities for people to talk about you with their own audiences.

Even small, local businesses can benefit from the online buzz. For example, Curtis Kimball operates The Crème Brûlée Cart in San

Francisco, and within three weeks of opening his business, he learned that customers were coming to him after reading about his cart on Twitter. Realizing the potential that Twitter offered to attract customers through word-of-mouth marketing, he created his own Twitter account (@cremebruleecart) and quickly acquired over 10,000 followers. Now he uses Twitter to post where his mobile cart is located each day and what the daily flavors are, and his followers wait for and share that information, helping him to build his business to the point where he quit his job as a carpenter to keep up with the demand. The Crème Brûlée Cart also has a page on Yelp, including hundreds of reviews, uploaded photos, and more.

Why Word-of-Mouth Is an Important Part of Social Media Marketing

Most small businesses get many of their customers from word-of-mouth promotion. Social media offers digital word-of-mouth to a global audience. Consumers have access to massive amounts of information, which they can access instantaneously and talk about with their friends and complete strangers whenever they want. Therefore, it's important that your business be active across the social Web, giving people reasons to talk about it. For many small businesses with limited marketing budgets, the word-of-mouth marketing potential of social media allows them to compete against larger businesses with deeper marketing pockets. It also helps businesses get to know current and prospective customers—something that small business owners are typically better equipped to do than executives and employees of large corporations, who are usually impeded by corporate and legal policies.

Small businesses can react faster to online conversations than big businesses can, and that's an advantage you should capitalize on. Keep track of the online conversations about your industry and business, and get involved in them. When you keep your business on the tip of people's tongues (or keyboards, as the case may be), they're more likely to talk about you. To learn how a small bakery generates an online buzz that has driven the business to new heights of success, see "Cakes for Occasions Generates an Online Buzz Through Social Media."

CAKES FOR OCCASIONS GENERATES AN ONLINE BUZZ THROUGH SOCIAL MEDIA

Kelly Delaney of Cakes for Occasions (www.cakes4occasions.com) may not have known anything about social media marketing when she started using Twitter, LinkedIn, and Facebook a year and a half ago, but that didn't stop her from diving in and getting results. In fact, Kelly started with a social media strategy that changed dramatically based on responses she heard from customers. To that end, the Cakes for Occasions strategy evolved to focus on the conversations that people *want* to have. For example, Delaney learned that when she posts pictures of customers' cakes, they love it and share it. Also, if she posts discounts, customers like it because they feel like they're in the know.

Today, Facebook is the primary social media marketing focus of Cakes for Occasions, and Delaney uses it as a tool for conversation. She shares what's happening in the bakery, posts pictures of the process of making cakes, and publishes pictures of the "cake of the week." The customer whose cake is named cake of the week also gets a sticker on his or her cake box, inviting them to visit the Cakes for Occasions Facebook page (www .facebook.com/cakesforoccasions, shown in Figure 16.1) to see it. Customers who become a fan of the page can share the picture with their own Facebook friends.

Figure 16.1 The Cakes for Occasions Facebook page

Delaney also uses Twitter to tweet pictures of great cakes. These are often picked up by the local Boston media when they search for news stories. While Delaney focuses on Twitter primarily on the weekends, her assistant posts to Facebook two or three times per day. Usually the posts are quick (she spends 10 minutes posting in the morning and another 15 minutes before she goes home), but Delaney believes her business has increased in retail by 24 percent in 2010 thanks to social media marketing efforts. She also states that she saved close to $10,000 on advertising costs alone over a one-year time frame, since she shifted much of her marketing efforts into social media.

"Word-of-mouth is what drives our business," explains Delaney. "Customers tell us they saw one of our cakes on Facebook at a party. We hear the stories all the time. Facebook also gives us testimonials, which are so valuable. We use Facebook to build relationships. It's personal to customers, because you're catching them at home. It's networking, not interrupting. Our Facebook page has over 1,000 fans, and it keeps growing. We post something, and four people usually respond. That's a 1 percent response rate. It's better than direct mail, and it's free! Decisions can be so costly in small business, but social media marketing is no cost."

Cakes for Occasions also uses social media tools for promotions, an approach that works very well in helping to spread the word about the business. For example, in January 2010, the "Pass Along a Smile, It's Contagious" campaign, which invited people to come into the bakery for a free smile cookie, was promoted only on the Cakes for Occasions Facebook page and received a huge response. Similarly, a promotion related to the 2010 Winter Olympic Games, which offered gold-medal cookies, was promoted on Facebook. In a contest tied in to the promotion, customers who spent $5 on Olympic merchandise were entered in a drawing to win a snowboard. Delaney was thrilled with the response rate and saw $5,000 in cookie and cupcake sales directly from the promotion. The Olympics promotion got an even bigger boost within a half hour of its announcement on Facebook: A customer came in for a cupcake and then posted about it on the U.S. Olympic Hockey Team page. Delaney's phone began ringing and continued all day. Cakes for Occasions was featured on the news, and all of the publicity and sales came from Facebook.

Delaney tries to use a variety of tools in her social media marketing efforts. For example, she created a promotion for people to become a fan of the Cakes for Occasions Facebook page, which included a global positioning system (GPS) tracking app that fans could use on their mobile phones or on the Facebook page to see where the Cakes for Occasions van was at any given moment. Fans were invited to come out to the van for a free piece of pie. The promotion lasted for one day only, and on that day, the number of fans of the Cakes for Occasions Facebook page grew by 40 percent. Delaney also used SurveyMonkey (www.surveymonkey.com) in a promotion tied to the Disney movie *The Proposal,* for which Cakes for Occasions was hired to create a cake. Delaney held a contest on Facebook that invited people to become a fan of the Facebook page and then submit their own proposal stories. The top three stories were published on the Cakes for Occasions Facebook page, and fans were invited to vote for their favorite, using a poll Delaney created with SurveyMonkey. Within one and a half days, 54,000 votes came in from 48 out of 50 states in the United States.

Delaney's advice to businesses looking to get into social media marketing is simple: just get started. "This is where your customers are, and you need to be there, too," she says. "A business owner would do *anything* to get customers in front of you in your store. With social media, you can get in front of customers who are listening on their own time. Sharing and interacting is worth so much more."

Sample 30-Minute Social Media Marketing Plans for Word-of-Mouth

Take some time to create a loose schedule of activities for your social media activities each day. Following are two sample plans to help you get started, and a blank Social Media Marketing Plan Worksheet can be found in Appendix C.

Word-of-Mouth Sample Plan A

METHOD OF PARTICIPATION	TIME	ACTIVITY
Content creation	15 minutes	Create and upload an interesting or entertaining video. Tweet it, blog it, and so on.
Content sharing	5 minutes	Share images on Flickr or Twitter with Twitpic.

(continued)

Word-of-Mouth Sample Plan A *(continued)*

METHOD OF PARTICIPATION	TIME	ACTIVITY
Connections	5 minutes	Write recommendations for others on LinkedIn.
Community building	5 minutes	Join forums related to your business, and actively participate.

Word-of-Mouth Sample Plan B

METHOD OF PARTICIPATION	TIME	ACTIVITY
Content creation	15 minutes	Create an online forum related to your business.
Content sharing	5 minutes	Invite other influential bloggers to write guest posts on your blog. Those who agree will probably write and tweet about their guest blog posts, too.
Connections	5 minutes	Add links to invite people to connect with you on Twitter, Facebook, LinkedIn, and so on in your e-mail signature, forum signatures, blog, etc.
Community building	5 minutes	Invite people to join your online forum by posting about it on Twitter, your blog, Facebook, LinkedIn, etc.

Chapter 17

Expanding Reach and Establishing Position

S ocial media marketing offers businesses the ability to get their messages in front of more people for a smaller investment than any other form of marketing does, meaning it enables businesses to expand the number of existing and potential customers they can reach. Instead of investing millions of dollars on prime-time television advertising, you can invest 30 minutes a day to reach a wide audience or a highly focused niche audience, depending on the activities you participate in and the conversations you join on any given day. Social media marketing also enables businesses to establish their market position, which is the place that brands, products, and businesses hold in consumers' minds relative to competitors in the same marketplace. Some of the best brands own a word in consumers' minds that represents their positions within their markets. For example, Cadillac owns *luxury* in the automotive market, while Hyundai owns *affordable*.

When your business joins the online conversations by publishing and

QUICK TIP

A niche audience is a highly focused segment of the larger audience. There are niche blogs, websites, social networks, and so on that cater to niche audiences, as well as niche groups within larger social networks like Facebook and LinkedIn. Social media marketing offers opportunities for businesses to connect with broad audiences, as well as with niche audiences through focused conversation and niche destinations.

sharing amazing content, making connections, and building communities, every communication, experience, and touch point becomes a representation of your brand and business. In other words, every single social media effort and activity helps position your business and brand in consumers' minds. When you own a position in consumers' minds, you have reached a coveted milestone in the world of marketing goals. Through consistency and persistence in efforts and communications, you can establish and retain your market position and further the reach of that position to a larger audience.

Why Expanding Reach and Establishing Position Are Important Parts of Social Media Marketing

In simplest terms, social media marketing enables businesses to accomplish three essential steps to growth:

1. Social media marketing allows businesses to stake their claim in the online space and within the online audience.
2. Social media marketing allows businesses to set audience expectations and prove their claims again and again.
3. Social media marketing allows businesses to deliver on those expectations and effectively retain their positions in consumers' minds.

No longer do businesses have to rely on expensive 30-second commercials or rarely noticed newspaper ads to grow. There is no limit on space or exposure on the social Web, except the limits you impose on yourself due to time constraints. However, as you've learned from the real-world small business social media marketing stories throughout this book, your business can find success on the social Web even with a small time commitment each day. The key is to acknowledge two important factors about social media marketing at all times:

1. Social media marketing is not about selling.
2. Social media marketing requires a long-term time investment that typically yields intangible rewards, but those rewards can compound and build a business exponentially.

There are really only two things that can prevent you from achieving some form of success through social media marketing: not starting at all and giving up too soon. To expand your business's reach and establish its position on the social Web, you need to be committed, but even a 30-minutes-a-day commitment can make a difference, as described in the sidebar "Mark Amtower Finds Success with LinkedIn."

MARK AMTOWER FINDS SUCCESS WITH LINKEDIN

Mark Amtower is a business-to-government marketing consultant who became an active LinkedIn user (www.linkedin.com/in/markamtower) in 2007. His LinkedIn profile page is shown in Figure 17.1, but he warns against printing a hard copy of his full profile. With more than 200 recommendations from his connections, you'd need a lot of paper to print it!

In just three years, Amtower learned so much about building a business through social networking that he added LinkedIn consulting to his list of business services. He sees his business pipeline filling faster these days than ever, and he attributes the vast majority of that growth to his activities on LinkedIn. In fact, Amtower shares, "When I network in person, people talk to me more about my LinkedIn activities than they talk about my Washington, D.C.–based radio show."

Figure 17.1 Mark Amtower's LinkedIn profile

Amtower's advice to people who want to use LinkedIn to build their businesses includes three main tips:

1. Be a specialist, not a generalist, and create a profile that highlights your expertise in your niche.
2. Give recommendations, and look for connections to write recommendations for you.
3. Leverage the question-and-answer section of LinkedIn, primarily in your niche.

Amtower also believes the group feature in LinkedIn is essential for building a business. He points out three tactics you can use to maximize your efforts and keep your name in front of group members:

1. Feed your blog to groups that allow the news link feature, so all members of the group can see your name and links to more of your expert content without any extra work on your part.
2. Post jobs to connect with people looking for career opportunities within your niche.
3. Join discussions, and make sure you post at least once a week on each group you belong to.

Amtower has successfully spread the word about conferences he plans to attend through LinkedIn group discussions. For example, rather than hiring a conference promoter, he got 70 people to attend one of his conferences (at $200 per person) simply from posting about it on LinkedIn and Twitter. However, Amtower is quick to explain, "Value-add is a big thing. You have to add value before you can get any kind of returns." He also mentions that social Web conversations move quickly, and you "need to add to discussions early. Lead conversations; don't wait and be last to join."

Amtower recommends that businesses have a strategy before they dive into social media marketing, with the understanding that social media marketing is a long-term commitment. For example, for three months before one of his social media seminars, he kept posting social media tips in all of the groups he belongs to on LinkedIn, which generated a significant amount of discussion. After those discussions came to fruition, he posted a message that invited people to attend the seminar in order to get all of his tips and more in one package. As he notes, "Every situation is not a selling situation. Social media is about visibility, credibility, and viability. If everything you put out there is selling, no one will want to hear from you."

Amtower keeps on top of what his competitors are doing on LinkedIn by running a search every two weeks on his competitors, partners, and customers and then benchmarking what they're doing. By crawling their LinkedIn connections, he finds new people to connect with and, sometimes, new customers.

In addition to building relationships, Amtower notes, social media participation can also boost efforts at search engine optimization, which can lead more people to find your business online. Mark reminds business owners that "social media marketing is not a stand-alone effort." To illustrate, he adds, "I integrate my traditional marketing with my social media efforts. Social networking should lead in-person networking to achieve a different level of success. They need to work together."

Using Syndication to Expand Your Reach

One of the benefits of social media marketing is the opportunity to get your content and conversations in front of a huge audience. Syndicating your content is another way to expand your reach, making it available to broader audiences. There are three primary forms of online content syndication:

1. **Free syndication:** Your content is republished on multiple websites without compensation.
2. **Ad-based syndication:** Your content is republished on multiple websites along with ads, and you may or may not receive a percentage of ad-based revenues.
3. **Licensed syndication:** Your content is republished on closed systems, rather than on the open Web, and you are paid royalties when your content is viewed.

Depending on your goals for your business, you may want your content to flow across the Web for maximum exposure. However, free and ad-based syndication services might put your content alongside inferior content, which could hurt your brand image. Only you can review free and ad-based syndication opportunities to determine whether they are a good match for your business, brand, and target audience. One of the most popular syndication sites offering free and ad-based syndication opportunities is BlogBurst.

Licensed syndication companies, such as Newstex, aggregate content from publishers that are typically editorially selected, meaning the content must meet quality standards. That's because content that is licensed for syndication is usually distributed to end users through closed systems such as corporate libraries and government databases. Professionals in fields like business, academia, journalism, government, and more use syndicated content for research to perform their jobs. Therefore, licensed syndication puts your content in front of a targeted professional audience, which may or may not be a good fit for your business. However, licensed syndication has few negatives from the perspective of brand expansion.

QUICK TIP

You can syndicate your blog, Twitter, audio, and video content to increase your exposure.

Sample 30-Minute Social Media Marketing Plans for Expanding Reach and Establishing Position

Start thinking of how you could spend 30 minutes each day participating on the social Web to expand your reach and establish your business and brand's position in consumers' minds. To guide your thinking, review the following sample plans. You can also use the Social Media Marketing Plan Worksheet in Appendix C to create your own schedule.

Expanding Reach and Establishing Position Sample Plan A

METHOD OF PARTICIPATION	TIME	ACTIVITY
Content creation	10 minutes	Record and upload an audio interview or podcast show.
Content sharing	10 minutes	Write guest blog posts, and share them with other blogs in your niche.

METHOD OF PARTICIPATION	TIME	ACTIVITY
Connections	5 minutes	Answer questions on LinkedIn.
Community building	5 minutes	Create a LinkedIn or Facebook group to represent your business.

Expanding Reach and Establishing Position Sample Plan B

METHOD OF PARTICIPATION	TIME	ACTIVITY
Content creation	15 minutes	Write an online article, and publish it on EzineArticles.com and other online article sites.
Content sharing	5 minutes	Sign up to syndicate your content, using a free or licensed service.
Connections	5 minutes	Make sure your business is listed correctly in Twitter directories such as ExecTweets and Twellow.
Community building	5 minutes	Publish a poll on your blog, asking for your audience's opinion on a subject related to your business.

Chapter 18

Direct Marketing and Promotions

Throughout this book, you have learned that success in social media marketing comes from building relationships, not from direct selling. In fact, you've been told repeatedly that self-promotion is generally unwelcome in social Web conversations. That is completely true. However, in Chapter 4, you learned that one size does not fit all when it comes to social media marketing, and as long as the vast majority of your social Web activities are *not* self-promotional, an occasional sales message won't destroy all of your work to date. Using the 80-20 rule, where 80 percent of your activities are not self-promotional and up to 20 percent are self-promotional, is a safe way to divide your time.

The key to successful direct marketing on the social Web is to make sure you're delivering the right messages and offers to the right audience and at the right time. These are the same guidelines you follow to develop offline marketing. In other words, make sure your messages add value to the online conversation instead of simply interrupting it, and make sure your direct sales messages are posted in the right places. For example, a florist that publishes links to her discount on baby arrival arrangements won't get the return she wants if those links are published in a Facebook group for singles and dating. Just having an audience you can reach for free doesn't guarantee they want to listen to you. Publishing an unwelcome message is the best way to ensure your future messages are ignored.

Why Direct Marketing and Promotions Are Important Parts of Social Media Marketing

There are many ways you can directly market your business using social Web tools. First, it's important to understand that direct marketing is any form of marketing that speaks directly to consumers in an effort to drive an immediate action, such as making a purchase or completing a contact form. In other words, the marketing effort triggers a direct response. Direct marketing can work on the social Web if your offers are presented at an appropriate time and to a receptive audience. Dell offers a great example. Among its uses of social media, Dell has an @delloutlet Twitter profile, where it publishes product discounts, generating millions of dollars in revenue from the orders that result.

QUICK TIP

Direct marketing and promotional messages published on the social Web should enhance the online conversation, not interrupt it or detract from it.

As with all aspects of social media marketing, there are no written guidelines to help you create a successful direct marketing program on the social Web. Even large companies are trying to figure out the best method to drive sales from the social Web. That means you're free to experiment and test different methods of selling your products and services through your social Web participation. For several tactics you can try for your business, see the sidebar "10 Easy Direct-Marketing and Promotional Tactics Using Social Media." However, you must continually analyze the effects of those efforts to see which appear to deliver positive results and which appear to do more harm than good. You can learn more about measuring results in Chapter 21.

Remember, direct marketing efforts can have a variety of goals, and you need to make sure you define your objectives before you self-promote on the social Web. For example, Lisa Skriloff of Multicultural Marketing Resources, Inc. had a goal to increase newsletter subscriptions. To achieve her goal, she started a LinkedIn group that dovetails with her business and helps to connect multicultural marketing experts with potential clients.

Since Skriloff's goal was to increase newsletter subscriptions, she decided to require that LinkedIn users request membership in the

10 EASY DIRECT-MARKETING AND PROMOTIONAL TACTICS USING SOCIAL MEDIA

1. Publish a discount offer on your social Web profiles like LinkedIn, Facebook, and Twitter.
2. Use the twtQpon Twitter application discussed in Chapter 8 to publish coupons on your Twitter stream.
3. On your business blog, hold a contest, and give away one of your products or a discount on a future purchase.
4. On your Facebook page, hold a contest, and give away a half hour of consulting time.
5. To boost your marketing contact list, offer a small gift on your blog in exchange for people joining your e-mail list.
6. Tweet limited-time offers such as "Visit our store in the next hour, and get 25 percent off any purchase."
7. Promote a tweetup at your brick-and-mortar location through Twitter. This works well for retailers, particularly for companies in the restaurant, entertainment, or hospitality industry, which can sell drinks and food during the event.
8. Share pictures of your products and services. This is particularly helpful to businesses that offer products people have to see to believe before making a purchase. For example, florists, interior designers, stylists, or home organizers could drive sales by sharing pictures of their latest projects and offering free consultations.
9. Publish discounts and sales offers on the LinkedIn and Facebook groups you belong to that are related to your business.
10. Create an "event" around your next sale, and promote your sale event across the social Web. For example, hype your event on Twitter using the Localtweeps Twitter application, as well as on LinkedIn and Facebook with the event applications available for those sites.

---

group. This allows Skriloff to send a personal message to new members when she accepts their requests to join the group. Skriloff's objective in sending this personal message is to make the new group members feel welcome and involved and allow them to know her better. In the message, she also invites recipients to sign up for her free e-mail newsletter, and she provides her direct contact information, so recipients can speak with her directly if they'd like to.

Skriloff has gotten a significant response to her personal e-mail, including an increase in traffic to her website and an increase in newsletter subscriptions. She says, "At least one-third of the people who receive my personal welcome e-mail respond to it. They share their story, ask questions, and initiate a dialogue with me. I respond by making suggestions for them to participate in the group, offer other resources, and tell them how they can use the LinkedIn group. Then I offer other services. My group has about 3,000 members, and every week, I get a handful of people who request more information. I started the group about two years ago, and my business has grown about 10 percent in terms of newsletter subscriptions alone."

Skriloff views her LinkedIn group as both a short- and long-term marketing strategy that integrates with her traditional marketing and networking efforts. She publishes information to her LinkedIn group and profile as well as to her Twitter profile and Facebook page but has found the most success (so far) through LinkedIn.

Skriloff offers tips to other business owners who want to use LinkedIn to build their businesses:

QUICK TIP

Don't just start a profile on Twitter or another social Web tool, publish a promotion or discount update, and expect people to respond. Short-term tactics won't deliver results unless you've already created a long-term strategy, worked to find your audience, and developed your band of followers.

1. Explore what LinkedIn has to offer.
2. Search LinkedIn by name, company, and group. Use keywords to find like-minded professionals.
3. Join relevant groups. You can join up to 50 groups and connect with more people. While you can only send direct messages to people you're connected to on LinkedIn, if you're in the same group as another person, you can send that person direct messages even if you're not connected to him or her.

Since social media is a real-time communications tool, it offers businesses the opportunity to create immediate-response marketing tactics. Instead of placing an ad in a magazine and waiting weeks for consumers to see that ad, you can publish a tweet and get a response within seconds. Many businesses take advantage of that immediate response by developing short-term promotions that are communicated through social media only. For example, a one-hour sale could generate a quick buzz and sales if you tweet about it to the band of loyal followers you've already spent time developing on the social Web. In other words, even the successes of short-term social media tactics depend on your long-term social media marketing strategy. To learn more about how a small business can effectively launch short-term promotions via social media, see "Boosting Gift Basket Sales with Promotions on the Social Web."

BOOSTING GIFT BASKET SALES WITH PROMOTIONS ON THE SOCIAL WEB

Debbie Quintana makes custom gift baskets that she sells at a website called Gourmet Gifts (www.thebestgourmetgifts.com). To find customers, she turned to the social Web and quickly learned that social media marketing "is not about how you want to operate. It's about what your customers want. We flipped our strategy and began thinking, 'What are all the ways people want to do business with us? Let's give it to them.'" Quintana's research and strategic thinking led her to use Twitter, Facebook, online video, Skype, and instant chat to build her business. "I want to make sure I'm everywhere," Quintana explains.

To save time, Quintana connects her social media accounts. For example, her tweets feed through Facebook, and she makes a list of everything she has to do each day in what she calls her 30-minute spin. "I only spend a half hour each day on social media so I'm not overwhelmed. You just have to be organized," Quintana says.

Quintana's direct promotions have helped her grow her business significantly. She uses live video to show customers their gift baskets and sends each customer the URL for the page showing that customer's specific basket, so each customer can view his or her basket before the design is completed. In the video on that page, Quintana spins the basket on a turntable and uses the opportunity to up-sell. As customers view what they'll get, they are allowed to switch components to create the final product they truly want. Quintana says, "It takes the mystery out of gift baskets and lets people customize their baskets." Quintana credits the live video, offered to customers who request it, for a 28 percent growth rate over the 2009 winter holidays. She promotes that service on her website's home page, shown in Figure 18.1. Quintana also takes orders through chat and instant messaging, which her customers love.

Figure 18.1 Customers of Gourmet Gifts can view live video of their purchases as their baskets are being assembled.

On Saturday mornings, Quintana puts a basket on live video and streams it to all of her social media profiles with a message that says she's taking orders on Facebook at that moment for the specific item at a special sale price. She also holds occasional "marketing blitzes," using every social media tool available to her on the same day to get her messages out. For example, she highlights her five best sellers on her website, giving people the ability to order one of those baskets with just two clicks. In one hour, she spreads the word about the offer across her social Web accounts, through e-mail, and on her blog. The effort has been a great success, bringing in numerous orders.

Quintana has moved all of her marketing online and says that unlike her results with traditional marketing, the return on investment she sees from social media marketing is massive. However, Quintana understands that social media marketing is a long-term strategy, especially in the case of Facebook, where building relationships and interacting over the long term are so important. Quintana explains, "The old way of doing business, you'd make a sale and didn't see or talk to the customer again. With social media, I stay active and stay in contact with customers over the long term."

Sample 30-Minute Social Media Marketing Plans for Direct Marketing and Promotion

Following are two sample 30-minute social media marketing plans you can use to create your own direct marketing and promotion activities. Be sure to check out Appendix C for a blank Social Media Marketing Plan Worksheet that you can use to develop your own schedule of activities.

Direct Marketing and Promotion Sample Plan A

METHOD OF PARTICIPATION	TIME	ACTIVITY
Content creation	5 minutes	Publish tweets about special offers or sales.
Content sharing	10 minutes	Request others to share your special offers on Twitter to earn a bigger discount.
Connections	5 minutes	Invite people to join your LinkedIn group for exclusive tips and discussions.
Community building	10 minutes	Post an update to your Facebook profile with an exclusive discount available only to people who *like* your Facebook page (meaning your page is included in their Facebook profile list of Likes). Blog and tweet about the special discount with a link to *like* your Facebook page.

Direct Marketing and Promotion Sample Plan B

METHOD OF PARTICIPATION	TIME	ACTIVITY
Content creation	10 minutes	Write a special-discount blog post.
Content sharing	5 minutes	Share links to your special-discount blog post on Twitter, Facebook, etc.
Connections	5 minutes	Reach out to potential new connections by inviting them to *like* your Facebook page to get a gift or discount code. You can do this by publishing an announcement on your blog, Facebook profile, Twitter, LinkedIn groups, in forums, and so on.
Community building	10 minutes	Offer free samples of your products to your connections, and ask them to write honest reviews on their blogs, Twitter, etc.

PART IV

Maintaining Social Media Marketing Momentum over the Long Term

Chapter 19

Integrating with Traditional Marketing

Despite what you might hear, traditional marketing is not dead. Social media marketing presents an incredible opportunity to meet more people and build deeper relationships than ever, but it's just one component of your overall business marketing plan. Certainly, it is warranted to shift some of your marketing budget from traditional marketing tactics to social media marketing efforts, but there is still room for traditional advertising, promotion, and market research in all businesses' marketing budgets.

The first thing you need to understand before you can create your marketing plan and determine where your marketing budget will be spent is the difference between traditional marketing and social media marketing. In simplest terms, traditional marketing includes all of the marketing tactics that businesses have been using for years to boost sales. These tactics can include advertising, direct mail, point-of-sale displays, event sponsorships, event participation, and promotions like sales, discounts, coupons, and sweepstakes. Traditional marketing tactics are typically communicated to consumers through traditional media sources—newspapers, magazines, in-person, television, radio, and so on. The vast majority of traditional marketing relies on one-way conversations where businesses *talk at* consumers. However, the audience doesn't usually have an option to *talk back* to businesses.

Social media marketing, in contrast, includes all forms of marketing executed using the tools of the social Web and communicated through new-media channels such as blogging, social networking, microblogging, photo sharing, social bookmarking, video publishing and sharing, and so on. At its core, social media marketing is built on conversations and relationships. Consumers are able to *talk with* businesses, and they can start or join a conversation at any time, since the social Web is an open environment. That means social media marketing relies on two-way conversations where user-generated content becomes more powerful than business-created content as messages spread across the social Web through conversations, content creation, content sharing, connections, and community building.

Traditional marketing and social media marketing differ in more ways than the medium and the method of communicating messages to consumers. Today, the best marketing plan employs tactics from both traditional and social media marketing to create a comprehensive marketing strategy. Review the following list of ways in which traditional marketing differs from social media marketing, so you can better understand how these two disparate marketing methods can complement each other:

- **Source:** Social media marketing occurs through self-publishing and user-generated content across the social Web, while traditional marketing occurs primarily through television, radio, print publications, outdoor events, in-store signage, and other old-school marketing campaigns.
- **Marketing:** Social media marketing leverages pull marketing, which means consumers *pull* information from businesses, and those businesses must proactively or reactively provide that information in order to meet those consumers' needs. In contrast, traditional marketing relies primarily on push marketing, meaning businesses *push* messages to consumers with the hope that those consumers will react or respond in a specific manner.
- **Cost:** Social media marketing requires a much smaller monetary investment than traditional marketing usually does.
- **Messages:** Social media marketing messages from businesses are typically subtle and indirectly communicated. Often those messages are communicated not by the business but by the online audience. Traditional marketing messages are typically generated by the business behind them.
- **Interactivity:** Social media marketing is highly active and invites participation and interactivity, which generates ongoing

conversations among multiple individuals. Traditional marketing usually provides one-sided messages, which are received passively.

Integrating Your Traditional Marketing with Social Media Marketing

Integrating a social media marketing strategy into your existing marketing plan has become essential for businesses to reach their full potential in the 21st century. In fact, it's an absolute necessity for survival in today's fast-moving marketplace. A well-executed social media marketing tactic has the power to change a business, because the online audience is large and influential. Businesses that will survive and thrive in the next 10 years are the ones that take the time to create an integrated marketing plan where one element feeds off of the next and all marketing efforts communicate a consistent brand promise.

That means your social media and traditional marketing tactics must work together for maximum effect. A fully integrated marketing plan eliminates all vestiges of silo marketing, where individual marketing efforts stand alone and completely separate from the next. The truth is that silo marketing is impossible on the social Web, because eventually, your social media marketing efforts will overlap as your audience shares and discusses your messages and business. Furthermore, your social media marketing initiatives don't die offline. A marketing plan that is not fully integrated will lead to consumer confusion and can actually hurt your business.

Follow these tips to ensure your marketing efforts are integrated with one another for maximum results:

- **Don't try to fit your traditional marketing efforts and messages into social media.** Instead, modify your messages and tactics to fit each channel. However, make sure they don't contradict each other. Trying to fit a square peg into a round hole won't work.
- **While you can interrupt with traditional marketing, you don't want to interrupt on the social Web.** Instead, you should enhance and add value. Surround consumers with branded experiences through traditional and social media.

- **Create your own social media destinations as the nucleus of your integrated marketing efforts.** For example, all roads, including your social media and traditional marketing efforts, lead to your business blog.

QUICK TIP

Make sure your traditional marketing messages tell people where they can find your business online. And once they find you online, make sure it's easy to find your business everywhere else you are across the social Web. Provide prominent links to your various branded destinations, so consumers can choose how they want to experience your brand and interact with your business.

You can also use traditional marketing to promote your social media marketing activities, and vice versa, so your efforts can feed off of each other. For example, you can advertise your blog to boost traffic to it or your Facebook page to increase the number of fans. Online advertising is an excellent tactic to raise awareness of and activity on your social media destinations. For example, if you own a florist shop, you can place an ad on a popular blog about weddings, inviting people to join your Facebook page for special discounts. Don't be afraid to get creative when you're merging your traditional and social media marketing efforts. To read about how out-of-the-box thinking can bring great rewards when it comes to social media and traditional marketing, see "Ford's Integrated Marketing Strategy Helps Rebuild the Brand."

Think of it this way: social media marketing is a very audience-centric communications channel, while traditional marketing is more of a destination-centric communications channel. When you create a traditional ad, your goal is to match your message with the destination where consumers will see it. However, on the social Web, you never know where your message could end up being seen, once it has been shared. That means audience members can make your messages their own, which empowers them to take ownership and become emotionally involved with the conversation. This is just one more shift in thinking that you need to make from traditional to social media marketing in order to develop a fully integrated and effective marketing plan.

Samsung Electronics America effectively integrated traditional and social media marketing efforts in 2009 with a campaign tied to the biggest sporting event of the year in the United States—the Super Bowl. Most companies with deep marketing pockets look at the Super

FORD'S INTEGRATED MARKETING STRATEGY HELPS REBUILD THE BRAND

After a series of financial problems virtually destroyed Ford's brand image in consumers' minds in 2009, the company decided to launch an integrated marketing plan to rebuild brand trust and business. Traditional advertising tactics such as television and print advertising were supplemented with a multipronged social media marketing strategy targeted at young, Internet-savvy consumers.

Ford chose 100 YouTube, Twitter, and Facebook users and gave them each a new Ford Fiesta car to use free for six months. The only requirement for participation was that users had to write about their honest experiences online. Ford allowed consumers to take control of the conversation. Participants published experiences, which were not edited by Ford in any way. The effort succeeded in generating a positive online buzz about Ford, and most of the published consumer reviews were positive. Furthermore, the traditional and social media efforts complemented each other to build greater awareness of and interest in the campaign and the brand.

Bowl as the coup de grace where they can roll out their cleverest and most attention-grabbing ads in the hope that people see those ads and talk about them. It's a huge investment with the potential for little in terms of return on that investment. However, Samsung looked at a Super Bowl commercial as just one part of a larger integrated marketing initiative.

Leading up to the game on February 1, Samsung created an entire marketing campaign around its multimillion-dollar 30-second ad buy during the Super Bowl pregame. The campaign, called "That's How I See It," promoted Samsung as the Official HDTV of the National Football League (NFL). The campaign was also promoted with television commercials and celebrity endorsements from NFL players, television personality Regis Philbin, and rock star Alice Cooper, whose own recorded videos and messages were published on the Samsung website.

To add an element of social media marketing to the integrated campaign, Samsung developed a contest inviting people to create their own videos showing how they enjoy preparing for and watching the Super Bowl. Viewers uploaded their videos to a special page on the NFL website, and visitors to the site voted for their favorite. The winner's video was announced on the website and in a traditional press release and was turned into the company's actual Super Bowl commercial. Concurrently, a Samsung mobile studio made stops at multiple NFL in-season games to record videos of fans responding to questions about what they like to do during the pregame. The various traditional and social media marketing tactics worked seamlessly together as a well-integrated marketing strategy.

Even traditional marketing through event attendance or sponsorship can include a social media marketing component. For example, Panasonic participates in the annual Consumer Electronics Show to generate a buzz about its products among show attendees, but in 2009, Panasonic wanted to take its efforts a step further by adding a social media marketing component to the traditional marketing of event participation. To that end, Panasonic turned to the blogosphere and recruited five influential bloggers to attend the show and blog about what they saw there, particularly about Panasonic, which paid for the bloggers' attendance and expenses. Participating bloggers were not required to write about Panasonic, but with Panasonic footing the bill for their trips, it wasn't hard to assume that they would, in fact, blog about Panasonic.

Influential bloggers have a wide online reach, which can have a significant impact on the online conversation and the spread of information across the social Web. Panasonic recognized that and allowed those influential bloggers to take control of the online conversation, knowing they wouldn't risk their own hard-earned reputations by publishing anything dishonest. Panasonic was also confident that the products it introduced at the 2009 Consumer Electronics Show were good ones that consumers would like, so allowing influential bloggers to freely write about those products (and more) provided two benefits: Panasonic earned some publicity for its products, and those five bloggers were able to publish useful and interesting information, thanks to Panasonic.

While Samsung and Panasonic used different tactics to integrate their traditional and social media marketing efforts, both methods delivered positive results and demonstrate that social media and traditional marketing work better together than apart. Of course, as you learned in Chapter 4, no two businesses are alike, and only you can determine through testing, research, and definition of your goals the best way to invest your marketing dollars and integrate your traditional and social media marketing initiatives.

Integrating Cross-Promotion Efforts

It is also important to integrate your cross-promotion efforts between your social media and traditional marketing tactics. Look for opportunities to promote your social media marketing activities in your traditional marketing messages and vice versa for maximum exposure. You should also cross-promote between your social media marketing efforts. For example, on your business blog, include buttons and links to draw attention to your Twitter, Facebook, and LinkedIn profiles, and invite people to follow or connect with you on your other branded destinations (see the example in Figure 19.1). Similarly, include your Twitter ID and blog URL in your marketing e-mails and advertisements. You should also promote traditional marketing efforts such as event participation or sponsorship through your Twitter profile, on your blog, on your Facebook page, and so on.

Figure 19.1 Prominently display links to your social media profiles and destinations on your business blog.

The bottom line is this: you can't assume that because a consumer typically communicates with you through a social media marketing or traditional marketing channel, he or she isn't interested in your other marketing efforts. Therefore, you should cross-promote your marketing efforts within your various social media activities as well as between your social media and traditional marketing initiatives. This ensures that your audience is aware of the various ways to connect with your business, giving them the chance to self-select how they want to interact with or experience your brand.

Chapter 20

Following the Rules of Social Media Marketing

To keep your participation on the social Web welcome and lawful, you need to be aware of several types of rules. These rules include laws as well as commonly accepted ethics and unwritten guidelines of Web 2.0. They should guide your own online participation as well as the way your employees join the online conversation. Remember, feigning ignorance won't get you off the hook if you violate a law, and the saying "It's better to beg forgiveness than it is to ask permission" (often attributed to U.S. Navy Rear Admiral Grace Hopper) doesn't fly on the social Web. That means the onus is on you to learn and follow both the written and unwritten rules of the social Web.

The chapters in Part II introduced you to a variety of social Web do's and don'ts, and this chapter will review a few of the biggest concerns, including copyright laws. For clarity, this chapter is broken into two sections. The first addresses written rules of the social Web—both actual laws and suggested standards for you to publish on your blog or develop internally for your employees. The written rules of social media marketing vary, but all are intended for one thing: to protect someone. That someone could be you, for example, or it could be a copyright owner. The second section of this chapter addresses the unwritten rules of social media marketing, including ethics, responsibility, and appropriateness of behavior.

Written Rules of Social Media Marketing

The written rules of social media marketing include laws created by the government, as well as disclaimers and statements written and published by you in order to create user expectations for your branded destinations and communications. Familiarize yourself with the various issues and concerns listed in this section to make sure you are abiding by the laws and protecting yourself accordingly.

Copyrights, Fair Use, and Creative Commons

In Chapter 10, you learned about copyrights and Creative Commons licenses. To recap, every published work, including text, music, images, and so on, is copyright protected by the original creator or publisher of that work. You cannot reuse another person's copyrighted material in your social media marketing efforts without first obtaining permission to do so from the copyright owner. There is a gray area of copyright law called fair use, which states that copyrighted work may be republished for educational purposes, to add commentary, for research, or for news reporting. However, fair-use limitations and allowances are debatable, so the safest course of action is always to seek permission to reuse another person's work within your own social media marketing efforts.

When you do copy even a portion of another person's work and republish it on your own blog, video, and so on, you should always cite your source. Even if you're only reusing a sentence from a larger written work, you should include a link back to the original source. Not only is providing attribution the right thing to do to keep you out of legal trouble, but it also puts you on the original source's radar screen because your attribution link could drive additional traffic to the original source. If the original source tracks how visitors arrive at his or her site, then your link will show up in the source's Web analytics reports. That means in addition to protecting you from legal trouble, attribution can help you to increase your own online following, particularly among an audience of influencers.

Creative Commons licenses were created in an effort to reduce the burden for publishers who want to discuss other people's published works or allow people to discuss their own works (see www .creativecommons.org). When a Creative Commons license is applied to a published work, the limitations related to republishing that

work are not as strict as a full copyright would be. You can review the six
types of Creative Commons licenses in
Chapter 10.

Trademarks

Businesses trademark names, logos,
and taglines in order to protect them.
For example, if a beverage company
launched a new product called Coke
tomorrow, the Coca-Cola Company would have a big problem with
that and sue for copyright infringement. That's because a trademarked
name is protected so only the trademark owner can use it within the
industry in which it is trademarked. Trademark laws were enacted to
ensure fair competition is allowed without customer confusion related
to names, logos, and so on.

With that in mind, you should trademark the name you use in
commerce and your social media marketing efforts to brand your
online presence. If you spend years building your online presence
using your business name, but that name isn't trademarked, you run
the risk of another company using that same name in your industry,
trademarking it, and sending you a cease-and-desist notice that says
you're infringing on its trademark. The worst scenario is that you have
to change your name, and all of the work you've done in terms of
brand building and search engine optimization around your name will
have been for naught.

Before you start to build your branded online presence, you need
to do three things:

1. If you don't already own the trademark for your name, do some
research, and find out who else is already using that name. Visit
the website of the U.S. Patent and Trademark Office (www.uspto
.gov), and conduct a search to see if anyone already owns the trademark for the name you want to use within your industry, as shown in
Figure 20.1.

2. If no one owns the trademark to your name, register for ownership of that trademark. Complete the registration form (which
requires a fee) on www.uspto.gov, or hire an attorney to help you register the trademark if you need help.

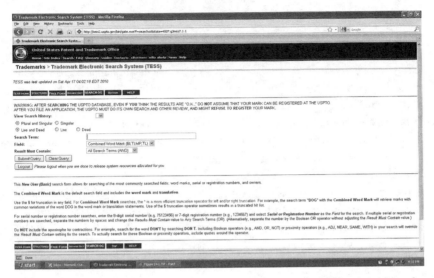

Figure 20.1   Search the U.S. Patent and Trademark Office database for trademark ownership.

3. Secure your name within your URL, Twitter profile, Facebook page, Facebook group, LinkedIn group, and so on. Even if you're not ready to build a complete Facebook page or LinkedIn group right now, you should still create accounts using your branded online name before someone else gets it.

Libel

Libel is any form of written or published words that are intended to damage another person or entity's reputation. While there are gray areas of the laws related to libel that say forms of satire are not deemed to be libelous, the safest route to take in your business's social media marketing efforts is to refrain from publishing negative comments about your customers, competitors, or business partners—or anyone else, for that matter. Not only would negative commentary hurt your brand image, but it can also get you in trouble with the law.

Laws Governing Reviews and Endorsements

You learned a bit about the laws related to online endorsements and reviews in Chapter 12, which included an introduction to Title 16, Part 255 of the Code of Federal Regulations from the Federal Trade Commission. If you publish or ask for reviews and endorsements of your products and services, you need to be familiar with the FTC laws outlined in the latest edition of the Code of Federal Regulations. (Visit www.ftc.gov or visit your local library to access the Code of Federal Regulations.) The most important thing to remember related to reviews and endorsements is that all compensation, including free products for trial, must be reported with the review, and the review must clearly state that it is written in return for that compensation as well as provide an honest evaluation of the product.

Site Policies

To protect yourself from potential problems and lawsuits, you should include written policies on your website, blog, and other branded social media destinations. For example, a privacy policy on your website and blog should tell visitors what (if any) information you collect about them when they visit your site and what you do with that information after you collect it. A policy for terms and conditions of use should include all of your site or blog disclaimers necessary to protect you, and a comment policy should set customer expectations related to conversations that take place on your blog.

QUICK TIP

Include links to your site policies in your website and blog footers (the static content at the bottom of your blog pages), so they're accessible from every page.

Policies can vary in length and tone based on your business and your audience. Depending on your business and online activities, you should consider hiring an attorney to help you craft site policies that fully protect you and your business. To get a general idea of the kind of information blog policies include, you can read the sample policies for privacy, terms and conditions of use, and comments in Chapter 7.

Guidelines for Employees' Social Media Participation

Employees can participate in social media in two ways: as an official representative of your business (for example, writing on your business blog or updating your business's Twitter stream) or independent of your business on their own social media profiles (for example, writing a personal blog or updating a personal Facebook profile). Therefore, you should have two distinct sets of guidelines for employees to understand and follow: an internal social media participation policy for participation on behalf of the company and an external social media participation policy for independent, personal participation.

Your internal social media participation policy should outline what employees are and are not allowed to say and do when they publish content to the social Web on behalf of your company. For example, they should refrain from publishing trade secrets or proprietary information. They should also avoid obscenities and arguments. To get started in writing your policy, review the employee social media participation policies of the following well-known companies:

- **IBM:** www.ibm.com/blogs/zz/en/guidelines.html
- **Intel:** www.intel.com/sites/sitewide/en_US/social-media.htm
- **Wal-Mart:** http://walmartstores.com/9179.aspx (policy for using Twitter)
- **American Red Cross:** http://docs.google.com/View?docid=df4n5v7k_216g5jdd7c8&hgd=1

QUICK TIP

If you do a Google search for "employee social media participation guidelines" or "employee social media participation policies," you'll find many examples from small and large companies. You can review these and use them as a foundation for creating your own policies and guidelines. You can also find links to a variety of social media policies in the Employee Blogging and Social Media Policy Directory on the Blogging page of About.com (http://weblogs.about.com/od/business blogging/tp/EmployeeBloggingand SocialMediaPoliciesDirectory.htm).

The important thing to remember when you're creating policies for employees' social media participation is to make sure that employees are not afraid to participate because of the excessive rules they're expected to follow. Instead, follow these tips for creating an effective policy:

1. Make participation easy and nonthreatening for employees.
2. Create a 360-degree loop of information sharing.
3. Be accessible for questions and problems.
4. Omit corporate rhetoric.
5. Allow employees to exude their personalities.
6. Enable employees to take responsibility for their social media activities.

Think of it this way: If Google can have more than 100 company blogs written by employees and thousands of additional employees participating independently on the social Web, then you can, too. Don't be afraid to let employees participate and share their love of your brand and company. After all, your own employees are your best brand advocates. Let them spread the word about your business across the social Web.

QUICK TIP

The Social Media Business Council offers a helpful Disclosure Toolkit at www.socialmedia.org/disclosure.

Unwritten Rules of the Social Web

Most of the unwritten rules of the social Web are rooted in common sense. In other words, if you act in a polite, inoffensive manner, then your participation should be welcomed on the social Web. Keep the concepts discussed in this section in mind during all of your social media marketing activities to ensure you don't earn an unpleasant reputation and are not blacklisted from participation on specific sites.

Don't Overpromote

The social Web is not a place for an abundance of overt sales messages. If you do nothing but sell on the social Web, no one will want to interact with you. Follow the 80-20 rule discussed throughout this book to ensure you're contributing and adding value far more frequently than you're self-promoting.

Don't Spam

Several of the ways in which you can participate in the social Web will cause you to be viewed as a spammer. Ignorance is not a valid defense. Instead, memorize the following 10 tactics that can get you labeled as a spammer, and avoid them at all costs:

1. Don't leave comments on blog posts that include nothing but a link to your site or a useless comment and a link to your site. All comments should add value to the conversation. Instead of including additional links in your actual comment, link from your name in the URL field of the comment form to your website or a specific page you want people to find.
2. Don't publish blog posts that are nothing more than an ad asking people to buy a product or service.
3. Don't tweet a link that leads people to purchase a product but offers no other useful information.

4. Don't send Facebook or LinkedIn group invites to people who are not in your target audience and would have no interest in joining your group.
5. Don't publish pages on your blog that include nothing but ads and links to purchase products but no other useful information.
6. Don't respond to Twitter follower announcements with an automated thank-you message that does nothing more than clutter the recipient's e-mail in-box.
7. Don't publish links to your website, blog, or products on forum discussions without adding any value to the conversation.
8. Don't leave the same comment on multiple blog posts, forum discussions, etc. for no reason but to get more links back to your own site.
9. Don't hire a link-farming company that offers to boost your blog or site traffic by creating an abundance of links through blog and forum comments. Many of these companies use automated systems to publish comments that are viewed as spam by blog owners, or they hire people to publish comments with no quality control, often causing the type of spam mentioned in the first rule.
10. Don't pay for text links (called *text link ads*), which can be viewed as a form of spam. Google and other search engines might penalize you if you're caught paying for or publishing text link ads.

Play Nice

Just because the social Web is a conversational, fun place to spend time doesn't mean you can completely let down your guard and speak without thinking first. Remember, your online conversations live for a long time and can spread very wide. For example, in April 2010, the Library of Congress announced it had acquired the entire archive of public tweets from Twitter dated back to March 2006. Avoid participating in negative discussions, name-calling, and other conversations that can reflect negatively on your business and brand. When in doubt, stay quiet. It can be hard to take something back once it's published on the social Web.

Acknowledge Other People

No man is an island on the social Web. Instead, there is power in groups and in numbers. That means you need to acknowledge oth-

TRUE STORY

Gary Vaynerchuk of the highly popular *Wine Library TV* video series and blog responds to every e-mail and social media comment directed at him every day. He cites that interaction and acknowledgment as one of the most important catalysts to his success in social media marketing.

ers by responding to them when they reach out to you. Whether they leave comments on your blog or Facebook page, send an @reply or direct message to you on Twitter, or send you an actual e-mail, you need to take the time to acknowledge those people in an effort to build relationships with them. Ignoring people on the social Web is the first step in destroying all your efforts at social media marketing.

Be Personable

The social Web is not a place for corporate rhetoric. In fact, publishing content and participating in online conversations using verbiage that sounds like it comes from a corporate policy brochure is a certain way to be ignored on the social Web. Talk to people as you would speak to them if they were standing right in front of you. Don't speak *at* people on the social Web. Instead, speak *with* people, and remember that what they have to say is even more important than what you have to say.

Be Honest

The social Web has created an environment where people can communicate faster and with more people than ever. As a result, consumers have lost much of the naïveté that they held in the past. Today, they can tweet a question about a marketing message and get answers and opinions from people around the world, telling them whether or not the message and the company behind the message are trustworthy. To be blunt, dishonesty on the social Web will be detected. You might not get caught immediately, but eventually, dishonesty will be rooted out, and the story will spread faster than you can say, "Sorry."

It's a risk that is not worth taking. Instead, be honest, open, and transparent in your social media marketing activities. You'll be rewarded for it in the long term.

Chapter 21

Measuring Results, Testing, Tweaking, and Trying Again

Before you invest time in social media marketing, you need to fully understand that quantifying the results of your efforts is very difficult. Few tools offer trustworthy hard numbers to calculate the return on investment generated by your social media marketing tactics. But that's OK. Remember, much of your success in social media marketing comes in the form of intangible benefits like brand building and relationship building. The success of social media marketing campaigns should be measured with regard to goals related to overall objectives, rather than actual net revenues generated by a campaign. You need to define your objectives for social media marketing and then assess the intangible and tangible results that stemmed from individual tactics to determine how successful those tactics were in helping you achieve your original objectives.

In other words, calculating return on investment (ROI) is the usual way in which marketers track the success of marketing programs, but for social media marketing, calculating return on objectives (ROO) is a better indicator of performance. Consider a traditional direct-mail piece, which costs a certain amount to produce and mail. The ROI on that effort is calculated by the response rate and sales generated from the mailing. How do you measure the ROI for social media conversations that happen on Twitter or Facebook? Those conversations are worth something. In fact, when it comes to long-term growth, those conversations are worth a *lot*. It's nearly impossible to calculate the ROI of conversations, but that doesn't mean they're not effective in building your business. Therefore, even though tools to measure the results of social media marketing leave a lot to be desired, that doesn't mean social media marketing shouldn't be an important part of your marketing plan. That is the disconnect that many corporate executives can't get over, and this is where small businesses can find significant opportunities to level the playing field, connect with consumers, raise brand awareness and loyalty, and grow.

While most companies still track website traffic as an indicator of social media marketing's performance, it's also important to measure soft metrics and the indirect value that your social media marketing efforts add to your business. Social media participation can also help your business with market research and customer service. The simple acts of listening and learning on the social Web help your business grow, just as tracking discounts and promotions does. That means the best way to analyze the performance of social media marketing is with a combination of hard metrics and soft metrics and an understanding that soft metrics are just as important (or more important) than hard metrics, given that social media marketing is a long-term marketing strategy.

PepsiCo and Dell provide excellent examples of changing the marketing mind-set from analyzing hard metrics only to analyzing a combination of hard and soft metrics. When Pepsi rolled out its "Refresh Everything" campaign in 2010, the goal wasn't specifically to boost sales by a predetermined percentage, but rather to enhance brand relevance and strength. Using traditional market research, Pepsi analyzed how consumers felt about the Pepsi brand after the "Refresh Everything" campaign launched. Pepsi created a fully integrated marketing plan that leveraged social media and traditional marketing tactics for the campaign, and combined traditional research performance analysis with social monitoring analysis, using tools to track mentions. Furthermore, Pepsi used traditional Web analytics tools to track website traffic and other hard metrics. The ultimate goal of the analysis was to determine the campaign's overall impact on the social Web audience, particularly in niche communities, making the entire campaign—from goal setting to tactical planning and from execution to results analysis—work together as an effective integrated marketing effort.

Similarly, Dell changed its entire outlook on the social Web and social media marketing very quickly after the debacle of 2007 described in Chapter 3. Not only did Dell find a way to save its reputation after a very public social media disaster, but the company also found a way to generate direct revenue from the tools of the social Web, specifically, through its @DellOutlet Twitter profile, which generated millions of dollars in revenue in just two years. Dell also understands how to build communities on the social Web. For example, the Dell TechCenter is an online destination for IT leaders and managers to socialize with Dell engineers. The community provides a place where visitors can ask questions and build relationships, and although hard metrics are lacking, Dell believes the community has reduced a variety of internal costs and sped up the closing of sales. In other words, the conversations and relationships born in the Dell TechCenter community deliver results that can't be quantified but can be evaluated in terms of soft metrics.

QUICK TIP

Some companies specialize in helping businesses track social media marketing performance. Some well-known examples are Radian6, Nielsen BuzzMetrics, and Cymfony. Depending on your budget and goals, you might benefit from outsourcing your efforts in social media marketing strategy and metrics.

What Should You Track?

For gauging whether your social media marketing efforts are working, the easiest thing to track is the traffic to your website, blog, or other online destination you use as the branded nucleus for your online presence. Using a Web analytics tool like the ones discussed later in this chapter, you can learn how people arrive at your website or blog, including the keywords they entered into their preferred search engines that brought them to your site and the specific sites that referred visitors to your site. For example, if you see a large increase in traffic to your website from your Facebook page,

QUICK TIP

As you analyze conversations across the social Web, don't just gather hard numbers to track performance. Instead, accomplish two things at once by also joining in interesting conversations related to your business as you find them.

then you can probably assume that something you're doing on that page is working. It's up to you to keep track of what's happening on each of your social media profiles and branded destinations, so you can recognize peaks and dips in your blog or website traffic and the potential catalysts for those peaks and dips.

Not only can you get an idea about whether or not you're meeting your social media objectives by analyzing traffic to your blog or website, but you can also keep tabs on the conversations happening about your business or brand across the social Web by tracking Twitter mentions, Web and blog mentions, and more. Following are several kinds of data you can analyze to determine whether or not your social media marketing efforts are helping you meet your objectives:

- **Website and blog referrers:** Using Web analytics tools, you can learn how visitors to your website arrive there.
- **Twitter mentions:** Various Twitter applications and Twitter's advanced-search function can help you analyze who is tweeting about your business and what they're saying.
- **Web and blog mentions:** Using tools like Google Alerts, you can keep track of conversations that mention your business or brand across the Web and the blogosphere.
- **Social networking conversations:** Conduct searches on sites like Facebook and LinkedIn to find mentions of your business or brand.

Tracking and Search Engine Reputation Management

Your analysis should also include a focus on search engine reputation management (SERM), which is the practice of ensuring that the results people see for your business when they conduct searches on Google and other search engines are the results you *want* them to see and accurately reflect your business's and brand's image and reputation. Therefore, it's important that you conduct Google searches using your business and brand name as well as your competitors' names, product names, and other industry-related terms your customers are likely to use when looking for the type of information, products, and services your business provides. Analyze the results that various searches return to you, and make sure the results related to your business accurately reflect your business. If not, employ search engine optimization (SEO) techniques to ensure that the right kind of content rises to the top of searches.

You can use the following five SEO tips to ensure that your best content has the best chance of ranking high in keyword searches related to your business:

1. **Keyword research:** Analyze keywords using tools like Wordtracker, KeywordDiscovery, or Google's free AdWords Traffic Estimator tool (https://adwords.google.com/select/TrafficEstimatorSandbox) to learn the best keywords to target and use in your online content to boost search rankings for those pages.

2. **Create content:** Create amazing content that people will want to read, talk about, and share in an effort to increase the number of incoming links to your site. Having more incoming links, particularly from high-quality sites, improves your search rankings.

3. **Using keywords:** Take some time to learn about SEO tips by reading expert suggestions on sites like SEOmoz.org. For example, use your keywords in your headlines, and use variations at the beginning and end of your content and within subheads in your content.

4. **SEO don'ts:** Avoid activities for which search engines penalize you, which can downgrade your search rankings. These include keyword stuffing, buying links, and hiding keywords.

5. **Build relationships:** Actively participate across the social Web, and build relationships. This will ultimately lead to more incoming links to your site as more people discover and share your content.

Tools for Measuring Success in Social Media Marketing

Although there is no perfect tool for measuring success in social media marketing, there are some tools that can offer you valuable insight to help you tweak your existing strategies and tactics to better meet your goals. Some of these tools give you actual hard-number metrics for tracking performance, and some permit a more subjective analysis of your social media marketing efforts. It's best to use both methods of tracking results to get a comprehensive picture of what is and is not working to help you build your business.

Some of the best and most commonly used tools for measuring the performance of social media marketing are described in this section. But remember, common sense is an equally effective tool for analyzing your social Web participation. If you can't get hard numbers to support the usefulness of your efforts at social media marketing, that doesn't mean those efforts aren't helping your business.

Conversation Analysis

Social media marketing performance can be tracked using a new form of ROI: Return on Impressions. There are two types of impressions to analyze. The first type is Web impressions, which is the number of times your brand is mentioned or seen by the online audience (similar to impression-based advertising) and affects brand awareness and recognition. The second type is perception impressions, which refers to the way people perceive your business and brand based on the conversations they read or participate in across the social Web.

Both of the new definitions of social media marketing ROI are rooted in conversations, which you can track and follow using a variety of tools, such as the ones described below.

GOOGLE ALERTS You can sign up for the free Google Alerts tool (http://www.google.com/alerts) so you receive e-mail updates when keywords of your choice are found online. Just complete the form shown in Figure 21.1. You should set Google Alerts for your business name, your brand name, and even your own name.

GOOGLE SEARCH Use the Google Advanced Search tool shown in Figure 21.2 to find content published about your business or key-

Figure 21.1 The Google Alerts form

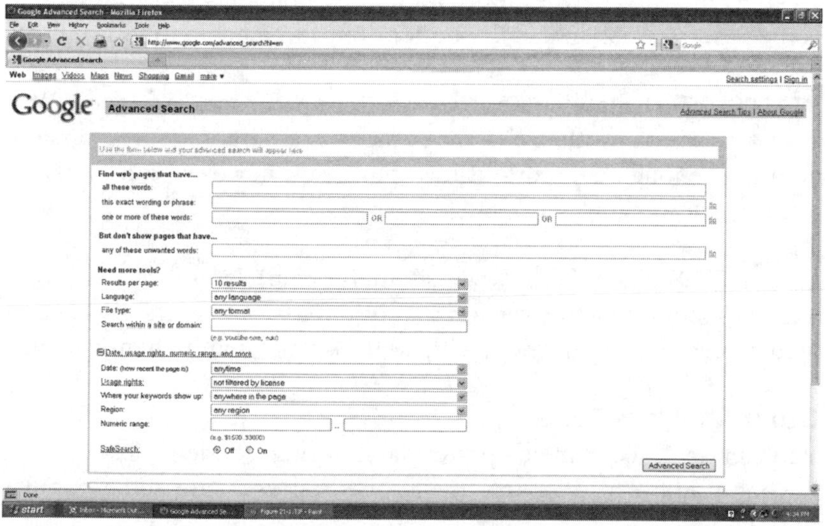

Figure 21.2 The Google Advanced Search form

words of your choice. Use the Date field in the Advanced Search form to conduct daily or weekly searches, so you stay on top of the online discussion.

TWITTER ALERTS Use a free Twitter application like TweetBeep, and sign up to receive e-mail updates when the keywords you choose are tweeted. Make sure you set up Twitter alerts for your business name, too.

TWITTER SEARCH Use Twitter's advanced-search tool (http://search .twitter.com/advanced), shown in Figure 8.2, to search Twitter for tweets that use the keywords of your choice.

Web Analytics Tools

To track hard metrics related to your blog or website performance, use a Web analytics tool like one of the options described below.

GOOGLE ANALYTICS Google Analytics is free and offers a wide variety of information related to the performance of your website or blog. You can get a detailed analysis of the traffic to your blog or website, as well as keywords people searched to find your site, sites that refer traffic to yours, top-performing content, and much more. I have used a variety of Web analytics tools, and in my opinion, Google Analytics is the best free tool. In fact, it's better than several paid tools I've used.

STATCOUNTER StatCounter (www.statcounter.com) is a good Web analytics tool that offers a decent amount of data in its free version. To access enough data for business purposes, however, you'll need to use the paid version.

SITE METER Site Meter (www.sitemeter.com) is also a good Web analytics tool with a free version that offers basic statistics. Businesses would need the paid version, which offers more comprehensive data.

Other Analytics Tools

You can track social media performance using a wide variety of tools beyond traditional Web analytics tools. Following are some popular options.

FACEBOOK PAGE METRICS When you create a Facebook page for your business, you can access analytics about traffic to your page. While these analytics are not detailed, the data can help you notice trends or the success of specific tactics.

TWITTER APPS A variety of Twitter applications can be used to keep track of the ongoing conversation on Twitter. Monitter, BackTweets, and Twitter Analyzer, discussed in Chapter 8, are just a few of the free tools that offer insight into your business's participation and opportunities on Twitter. There are also Twitter apps that can help you keep track of how many people retweet your blog content; these include TweetReach, Retweetist, and the retweet button from TweetMeme (www.tweetmeme.com). In addition, URL shorteners such as bit.ly (http://bit.ly) can help you keep track of how many people click on your links. You can find more Twitter apps and URL shorteners in Appendix B.

OTHER OPTIONS People use many other tools to keep track of social conversations. Keep in mind that these tools may not offer comprehensive or particularly accurate information, but you might want to test them to see if they can help you. These tools include Distilled's Reputation Monitor (http://reputation.distilled.co.uk), Social Mention, Samepoint, Whos Talkin, Twitter Grader, Website Grader, Blog Grader, and Facebook Grader. Don't forget: none of these tools are perfect, but they might offer you a nugget of information that can help you understand your social media performance or tweak your strategy. Just don't bet the farm on any of them. They are for exploratory research purposes only!

> **QUICK TIP**
>
> There are more expensive Web analytics tools, such as the tools available through Omniture. However, most small business owners find the free tools identified in this chapter adequate. Try a free tool first, before you invest in a fee-based tool.

Testing, Tweaking, and Trying Again

Just as no one knew overnight when the TV was introduced how to create television ads that motivate people to action, no one knew within 24 hours of the introduction of the first social Web tool how to create social media marketing tactics that draw a response. Remember, the word got out about Twitter in 2008. We're a long way from knowing how to use the tools of the social Web effectively to build businesses, but that doesn't mean we should stop trying. The truth of the matter is that there is no better place to experiment, test, and tweak marketing efforts than on the social Web, since the majority of your efforts require little or no monetary investment. The risk is so small that businesses would be crazy not to give social media marketing a try.

It's safe to assume that not a single company that has developed and executed a social media marketing campaign in the past hasn't learned from those campaigns and made changes to them for future initiatives. And they're still learning today. Even social media professionals continue to learn, and no one can claim to be a social media marketing expert—the social media landscape changes too quickly for anyone to claim that he or she knows all there is to know about it. That's what makes social media marketing so exciting. The opportunities are huge, and the barriers to entry are exactly the opposite. There has never been a better time to be a business owner with products or services to market, because the world is your oyster, and customers are available at your fingertips, thanks to the social Web.

Therefore, it's important to try each new social media marketing tactic with the understanding that it's unlikely to be perfect but you'll certainly learn something from it. As long as you continue learning, you can test new tactics, tweak your plans, and try again. When you see something is working, pat yourself on the back, and keep doing it. If you see someone else doing something you like on the social Web, try a similar tactic. There's no need to reinvent the wheel. As long as you're not plagiarizing content or violating any laws, the open Web is a place for people and businesses to learn from each other. Conducting competitive and market research on the social Web is a vital part of the learning process that you need to do in order to adjust your marketing strategy and tactics to achieve maximum success.

The social Web is an ever-evolving place, and what you're doing today on the social Web might not work tomorrow. You need to actively participate, listen, and continue to learn or you'll miss valuable opportunities. No one can keep up with all of the new tools and changes that happen on the social Web, so don't be discouraged if you feel as if you're falling behind. That's normal. Just keep on going and don't give up. That's the only real way to achieve success in social media marketing.

Chapter 22

Bringing It All Together

When it comes to using social media marketing to build your business, the worst action is no action, and your biggest problem is being invisible, not being talked about negatively. As long as you're part of the conversation on the social Web, you can hear what's being said about you and massage negative perceptions about your business. But if no one is talking about you, you have no chance for growth. That means you need to get involved on the social Web as soon as possible, not only to capitalize on the opportunities that it presents to your business, but also to develop and protect your reputation.

By reading this book, you've already taken the first step in leveraging the tools of the social Web to build your business. You learned what the social Web is and how it differs as a marketing medium from more traditional marketing, and you learned about many of the most popular tools for social media marketing. Your next step is to start accounts with some of those tools and test them out. You don't have to promote your social Web presence immediately. Instead, start a test blog that's not related to your business, and play around with it, so you have the chance to get comfortable using a blogging application before you launch a business blog. There is no timetable for social media marketing. As long as you get started, even if that means simply learning the tools, you're on the right path.

You also need to accept the fact that you might not have the time or budget to commit 100 percent to social media marketing today, and that's absolutely fine. As long as you join the social Web in some way, you're moving in the right direction. You can adjust the amount of time you spend on the social Web to meet your needs, goals, and interests. If you don't like Twitter, that's OK. Stick with the tool or tools you like for now. You can always add more tools to your social media marketing plan later. If you spend 30 minutes on social media marketing activities today but have only 5 minutes to devote online tomorrow, that's OK, too. You might even spend several hours writing an e-book one weekend and less time socializing during the week as you devote time to spreading the word about your e-book across the social Web. Again, the way you spend your time is up to you. As long as you're visible, active, and adding value to the online conversation, your efforts will be rewarded in terms of long-term relationships, brand building, and business growth.

> **QUICK TIP**
>
> It's better to spend one minute each day on your social media marketing efforts than it is to spend zero minutes on them. Each additional minute spent on social media marketing helps your business even more.

Starting Small

To eliminate the feeling of being overwhelmed by social media marketing, start small. That could mean you start a blog and write one post per week, or it could mean you start a Twitter profile and tweet for 10 minutes each day. Your goal should be to work yourself up to 30 minutes per day spent on social media marketing activities across varied branded online destinations. By testing, tweaking, and trying again, you'll learn which destinations attract the largest audiences or highly targeted niche audiences, as well as which destinations offer the best opportunities for developing relationships and conversations. In other words, as you spend more time on the social Web, you might change your strategy, abandon some destinations, or create new destinations. Since the social Web changes constantly, you need to be flexible and willing to change your strategy if your audience demands it. Remember, your goal is to build relationships and meet customer needs on the social Web. You need to listen carefully to your audience and respond accordingly, or they'll abandon you.

H&R Block offers an example of a company that changed its social media strategy to fit both its customers' needs and its own internal capabilities. After finding success on Twitter, H&R Block realized it needed to create a community-centric destination to answer customer questions in a better way than the one-to-one conversations on Twitter allowed. To that end, H&R Block developed the Get It Right question-and-answer online community, which replaced the company's standard blog and allowed a team of tax professionals to answer questions from, converse with, and build relationships with consumers. The site quickly grew to over 65,000 members and 1,000 tax professionals. While H&R Block understood that hard metrics would be difficult to track, the company believes the increase in brand favorability and customer service that the community offers exceeds actual sales goals.

The bottom line is that you shouldn't overthink things. Instead, go ahead and jump in, and start listening and learning on the social Web. Take the time to find out where your target audience spends time, and start hanging out on those destinations, too. Then join the conversation and introduce yourself. As you develop relationships and create a reputation for yourself on those destinations, people will begin to trust you. Once those relationships develop, you can bring those people over to your own branded destinations, such as your blog, Twitter profile, and Facebook page, where you can deliver more of your amazing content.

QUICK TIP

As hard as it might be, try not to think of your social Web activities as tactics to achieve business growth. Instead, look at your activities as opportunities to meet and help people. That's how you build relationships, and that's how you achieve long-term success with social media marketing.

In fact, much of that migration to your branded destinations will happen organically as you build more relationships across the social Web. Then those people will begin sharing your content with their own audiences, joining the conversation on your branded destinations, and talking about you.

That kind of earned media is priceless. Together, these activities lead to brand awareness and business growth. The amount of time required to achieve success in social media marketing depends on the amount of time you spend participating on the social Web and your ability to deliver content and conversations that people value. By analyzing responses to your efforts, you can tweak your activities in the future to achieve greater success.

Spreading Your Wings and Your Content

Earlier in this chapter, you learned that each business owner must follow his or her own path to find social media success because no two businesses are alike, but just as no two businesses are alike, neither are any two people on the social Web. In other words, the person who is actually *doing* social media marketing for your business is unique. To understand, consider Twitter. It is an incredible social media marketing tool, but only a small percentage of Twitter users account for the vast majority of Twitter updates. That's because Twitter isn't for everyone, which tells you that business owners with limited time and limited budgets need to pick and choose the social media marketing activities they will devote their time to.

If you devote your time to the activities that most interest your audience *and* interest you (meaning you enjoy using those tools and interacting on those sites), then you're more likely to be successful, faster. If you really don't like Twitter, that's OK. Don't market scared and devote all of your time to Twitter just because your competitor does. If you don't enjoy it, that apathy or dislike will show through in your online conversations. However, if you choose a tool that your audience uses *and* you enjoy, you're more likely to use it frequently, and your content and conversations will undoubtedly be more interesting, engaging, and passionate. That's what keeps people coming back for more.

The best-case scenario and your ultimate goal for social media marketing should be one that enables you to create branded destinations across the social Web centered around a primary social Web nucleus (see Figure 22.1), so your audience can self-select where and how they want to interact with you. For example, some people enjoy reading 140-character updates, while others want a more comprehensive blog post. Others might prefer watching a video over reading text. A full-blown social media marketing strategy includes all elements with a focus on those that deliver the best results in terms of building relationships and word-of-mouth marketing buzz.

Getting Started Right Now

When you put this book down, you are ready to join the social Web, but before you do, take a few minutes to read through the following

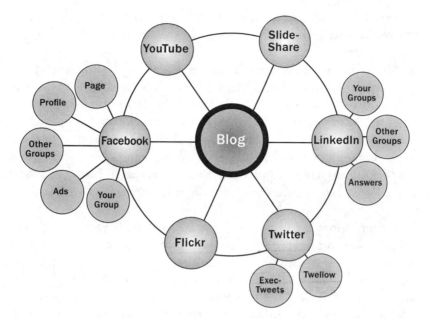

Figure 22.1 A blog is the nucleus of this sample business's social media presence.

Getting-Started Plan. If you start down a path on the social Web and hate what you're doing, change things around. Just as you change networking and conversational approaches in person, you can do so on the social Web. The only differences are that on the social Web, you're talking through your keyboard, and your potential audience is much, much larger.

GETTING-STARTED PLAN

1. Determine your goals: What do you want to get out of your social Web participation? Why are you doing it? Are you trying to generate direct sales? Are you trying to offer a form of customer service? Do you want to build relationships with customers and boost loyalty? Your answers to these questions greatly affect the type of content you publish and the activities you participate in on the social Web.

2. Evaluate your resources: Who is going to create your content? Who is going to maintain your social media accounts? Who is going to respond to questions and be the face of your business online? Do you have the technical ability in-house to join the online conversation? If not, are you willing to learn? Can you or someone who works with you write well? You need to be sure you have the necessary people in place to execute a social media marketing plan before you start.

3. Know your audience: Where does your target audience spend time online? What kind of content and conversations do the audience members get most vocal about? What kind of information do they want from you? What do they dislike? Remember, you're not just publishing marketing messages on the social Web. You need to find out what your audience wants and needs, so you can provide the kind of content they find useful and interesting. However, you also need to be personable, so they actually want to interact with you.

4. Create amazing content: Once you know where your audience spends time and what kind of content audience members want, take the time to give them more of that kind of content. Don't give up. You need to continually offer your audience amazing content, which also comes in the form of conversations, in order to build a loyal following of people who trust you as a source that can meet their needs and expectations.

5. Integrate your marketing efforts: All of your efforts at social media marketing should feed off each other. Cross-promote your efforts both online and offline, and make sure your social media and traditional marketing efforts work together seamlessly.

6. Create a schedule: Allocate specific times during your day to devote to social media marketing. For example, spend five minutes on Twitter before you check your e-mail each day and another five minutes before you leave work each day. When you create a schedule, it's easier to stick to it and make sure you don't skip your social media marketing activities each day. Use the Social Media Marketing Plan Worksheet in Appendix C to create your own daily schedules.

7. Don't forget the 80-20 rule: Always spend at least 80 percent of your time on social media activities that are not self-promotional and no more than 20 percent of your time on self-promotional activities.

8. Focus on quality, not quantity: It can be easy to get caught up in the numbers, but don't become a slave to followers and subscribers. It's better to have 1,000 highly engaged, loyal followers than 10,000 followers who sign up to follow you but then never acknowledge you again.

9. **Give up control:** You must let your audience take control of the online conversation and make it their own so they develop an emotional attachment to you, your brand, and your business. Remember, on the social Web, apathy or invisibility is a bigger problem than negativity.

10. **Keep learning:** You can never stop listening and learning. For success in social media marketing, you need to be flexible and accept that change is good.

> **QUICK TIP**
>
> Take a week to create accounts on each of the major social Web tools, including Twitter, Facebook, and LinkedIn. (See Chapter 6 for a handy list of URLs for the most popular social Web tools.) Poke around and discover the features of each. Also, create a business blog. If you need help, hire a freelancer, using one of the freelance websites listed in Chapter 7 to connect with a blog designer who can create your blog at an affordable price.

More Sample 30-Minute Social Media Marketing Plans

Part III offered several sample plans for 30-minutes-a-day social media marketing, and this section provides several more plans. Each plan demonstrates how the owner of a specific type of small business could spend 30 minutes on the social Web to build his or her businesses through brand building, word-of-mouth marketing, direct promotions, and more. Check out these plans for fictitious small businesses to get ideas for marketing your own business on the social Web.

Direct Promotion: 30-Minute Social Media Marketing Plan for a Florist (Twitter Focus)

Imagine you are a florist who wants to build her business through direct promotion through social media marketing. This 30-minute social media marketing plan helps you focus on Twitter to achieve that goal.

- **10 minutes:** Take pictures of your best arrangement each day, and post them to your Twitter profile using Twitpic the following morning. Use twtQpon to offer a discount to anyone who orders the same arrangement in the next 24 hours. Your Twitter updates should already be set up to feed into your Facebook and LinkedIn profiles, groups, pages, and so on, so the promotion is automatically published on those destinations, too.

- **5 minutes:** Write a blog post about your promotion, including the picture of the best arrangement.
- **10 minutes:** Midday, spend time responding to tweets related to your promotion, retweet other great content from other people, and respond to any other direct messages or @replies. Remind people about the promotion by retweeting your original post.
- **5 minutes:** End of business, respond to tweets, and retweet the promotion one more time. Also, retweet interesting content from other people, and tweet a useful daily tip or idea for your followers to learn from and share with their own followers.

Brand Building and Establishing Position: 30-Minute Social Media Marketing Plan for a Massage Therapist (E-Book Focus)

Imagine you are a massage therapist who wants to build your brand and establish your brand position through social media marketing. The plan focuses on e-book creation. It requires that you spend several hours (or hire a writer) writing an e-book about massage therapy that is helpful to people looking for a source for relaxation, stress relief, pain relief, or another goal that makes people seek the services of a massage therapist. The e-book needs to be helpful and explain how massage can benefit the reader. It can also indirectly promote your massage therapy services. It should include links to your website, blog, Twitter profile, Facebook profile, and so on. It should also be copyrighted using a Creative Commons Attribution license to encourage readers to share it with as many people as possible.

- **10 minutes:** Publish a blog post that promotes the e-book and explains how people can benefit from reading it. Include a link for people to download and read the e-book in PDF format. There should be no requirement for downloading the e-book (for example, no request for e-mail addresses), and readers should be encouraged to share it via e-mail or online with anyone they believe can benefit from it.

- **5 minutes:** Tweet about the e-book, and include a link to access the e-book. Take a few minutes to retweet other interesting content and respond to @replies, too. Your Twitter stream should already be set up to feed into your Facebook and LinkedIn profiles. Use an application like Localtweeps.com or Nearby Tweets to find people in your area. Follow them. Many will follow you in return, and you can tweet about your e-book again to reach a local audience, too. (*Note:* An even better approach would be to have found local people to follow on Twitter *before* you launched your e-book.

- **5 minutes:** Provide the link to your e-book in any Facebook and LinkedIn groups you belong to whose members might be interested in your e-book.

- **5 minutes:** Reach out to other bloggers or BlogTalkRadio show hosts whose audiences might be interested in your content. Comment on some related posts on other blogs with a link to your free e-book, and send an e-mail to the bloggers and show hosts, offering your time for a guest post or interview.

- **5 minutes:** Add the link to your e-book in your forum signatures, social networking profiles, and e-mail signature.

Word-of-Mouth Marketing: 30-Minute Social Media Marketing Plan for a Restaurant (Online Video Focus)

In this scenario, pretend that you own a restaurant and want to generate word-of-mouth marketing using online video.

- **15 minutes:** Record a video demonstrating how to make an appetizer or the "drink of the house." Alternately, record a video that teaches something, such as how to pair a wine with a specific food. Both options would be perfect for an ongoing video series.

- **10 minutes:** Upload your video to your YouTube channel, and blog about it. Make sure the video is uploaded for anyone to see, share, link to, and embed in his or her own sites and blogs. Embed the video in a post on your blog and on any other pages or sidebars on your website, blog, Facebook profile, Facebook page, and other social media where people can see it.

- **5 minutes:** Publish a Twitter update about your video. Your Twitter updates should already feed into your LinkedIn and

Facebook profiles, so they're updated, too. Also, share the link in relevant Facebook and LinkedIn groups and in related forums.

Indirect Marketing and Relationship Building: 30-Minute Social Media Marketing Plan for a Motorcycle Repair Shop (Facebook Page Focus)

Imagine that you own a motorcycle repair shop and want to indirectly build your business and relationships through Facebook. This plan requires that you have already created a Facebook page for the business.

- **5 minutes:** Send page recommendations to all of your Facebook connections. Tweet about your new Facebook page, and ask people to *like* your page so they can access helpful tips, discounts, and information available exclusively through your page.
- **10 minutes:** Write a blog post announcing your new Facebook page on your blog, and add a Like link on your website and blog and an additional link to access your Facebook page anywhere else you can (for example, your e-mail signature, forum signatures, Facebook profile, and LinkedIn profile). Also, add other Facebook social plugins to your website and blog sidebars.
- **5 minutes:** Upload pictures from your shop, and add them to your Facebook page, so people can get to know you, your employees, and your shop.
- **10 minutes:** If you have recorded any interviews with customers (for example, describing what his or her motorcycle means to him or her or how important a repair was to keep the bike going), you can upload a video to your YouTube channel and share the link on your Facebook page, as well as on your Twitter profile, blog, and so on.

There are so many ways you can build your business using the tools of the social Web. Each of these 30-minute sample plans could be revised dozens of ways and still elicit positive effects on the businesses implementing them. Remember, there is no wrong or right way to participate on the social Web to grow your business. As long as you follow the law and the ethics of the social Web, you can try a variety of creative marketing efforts. Just pay attention to your audience's reactions to your efforts to ensure you do more of the tactics people respond to positively and change or omit the tactics that people respond to apathetically or negatively. Above all, try to have fun!

The Final Word

In Chapter 2, I revealed the most important lesson you can take away from reading this book:

> *Social media marketing offers the single largest opportunity for entrepreneurs, small businesses, midsize companies, and large corporations to build their brands and their businesses.*

If you've made it this far, you've learned everything you need to know in order to dive into the social Web conversation to grow your own business, and you've realized that you really can achieve success at social media marketing in just 30 minutes a day. You also learned the second most important lesson revealed in this book:

> *When it comes to social media marketing, the worst action is no action at all.*

Ten years ago, business owners would have done anything to get a huge audience of consumers in front of them so they could talk to that audience. Today, all it takes is logging into the Internet and spending some time on the social Web. The best part is that it's free. What are you waiting for? Put down this book and get online!

I'll see you on the social Web.

Twitter Cofounder Biz Stone Reflects on Twitter in 2009

Written by Biz Stone. Originally published in the Times of London, England *(TimesOnline.co.uk) on December 27, 2009, and reprinted with permission from Twitter.com.*

On June 15, our technicians told me to add a note to our website. The note warned users of a planned maintenance session that meant our service would be inaccessible while we carried out an overdue system upgrade.

Immediately, we began to see a reaction in the form of tweets. Then came the emails. Then came the phone calls. Even the US State Department contacted us. The message was loud and clear: Twitter cannot rest while there is unrest in Iran.

However, if this maintenance was not done quickly, our operations team feared that the service might go down for days.

With the whole team on edge, my colleague Jessica Verrilli and I called our head of operations to convince him to do what was deemed extremely difficult if not impossible—reschedule the maintenance.

A few more phone calls and we had a consensus to postpone the work despite the risk. After all, this wouldn't be the first time we had to ask our engineers to perform the impossible. In the space of a year, user accounts had grown by a factor of 10 while our 45-strong team remained crowded into a loft space in San Francisco's industrial SoMa district.

The work was moved and the maintenance was eventually successful. In the days that followed, our service became inextricably linked to the Iranian election protests in hundreds of media reports on television, online, and in the newspapers.

Requests to discuss the tumult flooded in from everywhere but we did not engage. We chose instead to issue a simple statement on Twitter's blog.

While it is our job to keep the service running, it was not the appropriate time or circumstance to put ourselves into the same conversation with people who were risking their lives on the streets of Tehran. The experience remains a humbling one that would define the year for Twitter and also underscore the motivation behind a decade of effort leading up to this point.

My cofounder Evan Williams and I have spent the past 10 years developing large systems that allow people to express themselves and communicate openly. We are united in our belief that software has the ability to augment humanity in productive and meaningful ways.

Although we are already a few years into our latest collaboration, this has been the year the world took note of a simple service that has profound promise. For us, it has been a year during which we realised that no matter how sophisticated the algorithms get, no matter how many machines we add to the network, our work is not about the triumph of technology, it is about the triumph of humanity.

Many people have assumed that Twitter is just another social network, some kind of micro-blogging service, or both. It can be these things but primarily Twitter serves as a real-time information network powered by people around the world discovering what's happening and sharing the news. The Iranian election was the most discussed issue on Twitter in the final year of a decade defined by advancements in information access.

In the new year, Twitter will begin supporting a billion search queries a day. We will be delivering several billion tweets per hour to users around the world. These are figures we did not anticipate when we founded the company in 2007.

Looking back, the year is a blur, but that one summer morning remains fixed in my memory because it is a powerful reminder of why we find it meaningful to develop technology.

Resources and Help

Blogging Applications and Tools

b2evolution: http://b2evolution.net
Blogger: www.blogger.com
ExpressionEngine: http://expressionengine.com
LiveJournal: www.livejournal.com
Movable Type: www.movabletype.com
Posterous: http://posterous.com
Tumblr: www.tumblr.com
TypePad: www.typepad.com
Vox: www.vox.com
WordPress blog hosting: www.wordpress.com
WordPress blogging application: www.wordpress.org
WordPress plugins: http://wordpress.org/extend/plugins
Xanga: www.xanga.com

Web Hosts

BlueHost: www.bluehost.com
DreamHost: www.dreamhost.com
Go Daddy: www.godaddy.com
HostGator: www.hostgator.com
Just Host: www.justhost.com

WordPress Themes

DIYthemes: http://diythemes.com (premium)
eBlog Templates: www.eblogtemplates.com (free)
ElegantThemes: www.elegantthemes.com (premium)
FreeWordPressThemes.com: www.freewordpressthemes.com
   (free)

iThemes: http://ithemes.com (premium and customization)
StudioPress: www.studiopress.com (premium)
WooThemes: www.woothemes.com (premium)
WordPress Themes: www.wpthemesfree.com (free)

Blogger Templates

Blogger Buster: http://designs.bloggerbuster.com (free)
BTemplates: http://btemplates.com (free)
eBlog Templates: www.eblogtemplates.com (free)
pYzam: http://www.pyzam.com/bloggertemplates (free)

Movable Type and TypePad Templates

iThemes: http://ithemes.com/movable-type (premium)
PixelMill: http://www.pixelmill.com/products/website-templates/
typepad-templates.aspx (premium)

Free Images

Dreamstime: www.dreamstime.com
FreeFoto.com: www.freefoto.com
morgueFile: www.morguefile.com
PicApp: www.picapp.com
Stock.XCHNG: www.sxc.hu

Microblogging Tools

Jaiku: www.jaiku.com
Plurk: www.plurk.com
Twitter: www.twitter.com

Twitter Backgrounds

SocialIdentities: www.custombackgroundsfortwitter.com
TwitBacks: www.twitbacks.com
TwitrBackgrounds: www.twitrbackgrounds.com
TwitterBackgrounds.org: www.twitterbackgrounds.org
Twitter-Backgrounds.net: www.twitter-backgrounds.net

Twitter Apps

BackTweets: www.backtweets.com
ChirpCity: www.chirpcity.com
ExecTweets: www.exectweets.com
FileTwt: www.filetwt.com
FutureTweets.com: www.futuretweets.com

GeoFollow: www.geofollow.com
HootSuite: www.hootsuite.com
Localtweeps: www.localtweeps.com
Monitter: www.monitter.com
Nearby Tweets: www.nearbytweets.com
Retweetist: www.retweetist.com
SocialOomph: www.socialoomph.com
Topify: www.topify.com
Twazzup: www.twazzup.com
Tweet Scan: www.tweetscan.com
TweetBeep: www.tweetbeep.com
TweetDeck: www.tweetdeck.com
TweetMeme: www.tweetmeme.com
TweetPhoto: www.tweetphoto.com
TweetReach: www.tweetreach.com
TweetStats: www.tweetstats.com
Twellow: www.twellow.com
twhirl: www.twhirl.org
Twimailer: www.twimailer.com
TwitLonger: www.twitlonger.com
Twitpic: www.twitpic.com
Twitter Analyzer: www.twitteranalyzer.com
TwitterContd: www.twittercontd.com
Twitterfeed: www.twitterfeed.com
twtQpon: www.twtqpon.com
Twtvite: www.twtvite.com
WeFollow: http://wefollow.com
yfrog: www.yfrog.com

URL Shorteners
bit.ly: http://bit.ly
Cligs: http://cli.gs
Ow.ly: http://ow.ly/url/shorten-url
Short.ie: http://short.ie
SnipURL: www.snurl.com
TinyURL.com: http://tinyurl.com

Social Networking Sites
Bebo: www.bebo.com
Facebook: www.facebook.com
Google Buzz: www.google.com/buzz

LinkedIn: www.linkedin.com
MySpace: www.myspace.com
Ning: www.ning.com
orkut: www.orkut.com

Social Icons, Buttons, and Badges

Free Icons Download: http://www.freeiconsdownload.com/Free
_Web_Icons.asp
IconArchive: http://www.iconarchive.com/category/social-net
work-icons.html
My Social Buttons: www.mysocialbuttons.com
Twitter Buttons: www.twitterbuttons.com
Web Design Ledger: http://webdesignledger.com/freebies/the
-best-social-media-icons-all-in-one-place (links to hundreds
of social media icons gathered in one place)

Social Bookmarking Sites

Delicious: www.delicious.com
Digg: www.digg.com
Newsvine: www.newsvine.com
Propeller: www.propeller.com
Reddit: www.reddit.com
Slashdot: www.slashdot.com ("news for nerds and stuff that
matters")
Sphinn: www.sphinn.com (for search engine and Internet mar-
keting professionals)
StumbleUpon: www.stumbleupon.com
Yahoo! Buzz: http://buzz.yahoo.com

Image-Sharing Sites

Flickr: www.flickr.com
Photobucket: www.photobucket.com
Picasa: www.picasa.com

Video-Sharing Sites

blip.tv: www.blip.tv
Dailymotion: www.dailymotion.com
TubeMogul.com: www.tubemogul.com
Viddler: www.viddler.com
Vimeo: www.vimeo.com
YouTube: www.youtube.com

Podcast and Online Talk Show Sites

BlogTalkRadio: www.blogtalkradio.com
Blubrry: www.blubrry.com
Podbean.com: www.podbean.com

Online-Forum-Building Tools

phpBB: www.phpbb.com
Simple:Press: http://simple-press.com (WordPress forum plugin)
vBulletin: www.vbulletin.com

Freelancer Sites

CrowdSpring: www.crowdspring.com
Elance: www.elance.com
Freelancer.com: www.freelancer.com
FreelanceSwitch: www.freelanceswitch.com
Guru: www.guru.com
iFreelance: www.ifreelance.com
oDesk: www.odesk.com
ProBlogger job board: http://jobs.problogger.net

Blogging Help Sites

About.com Blogging page: http://weblogs.about.com
Blog Herald: www.blogherald.com
Blogger: http://www.google.com/support/blogger/?hl=en
Blogger Buster: www.bloggerbuster.com (blogger help only)
Blogging Pro: www.bloggingpro.com
Daily Blog Tips: www.dailyblogtips.com
Performancing: www.performancing.com
ProBlogger: www.problogger.net
TypePad: http://help.sixapart.com/tp/us
WordPress blog hosting: http://en.support.wordpress.com
WordPress blogging application: http://codex.wordpress.org/
  Main_Page
wpmods: www.wpmods.com (WordPress help only)

Microblogging Help Sites

About.com Blogging page: http://weblogs.about.com
Pistachio Consulting: http://pistachioconsulting.com
TwiTip: www.twitip.com
Twitter: http://twitter.com/help/start

Social Networking Help Sites
All Facebook: www.allfacebook.com
Facebook: http://www.facebook.com/help/?ref=pf
LinkedIn: http://learn.linkedin.com
MySpace: http://faq.myspace.com/app/home

Search Engine Optimization Help Sites
Search Engine Journal: www.searchenginejournal.com
Search Engine Land: http://searchengineland.com
SEOmoz: www.seomoz.org

Local Search Sites and Directories
CitySearch: www.citysearch.com
DexKnows: www.dexknows.com
Google Places: www.google.com/local/add
Kudzu: www.kudzu.com
Yelp: www.yelp.com

Books
Blogging All-in-One for Dummies, by Susan Gunelius. Hoboken, NJ: Wiley, 2010.

The Complete Idiot's Guide to WordPress, by Susan Gunelius. New York: Alpha, 2011.

Crush It! by Gary Vaynerchuk. New York: HarperStudio, 2009.

Google Blogger for Dummies, by Susan Gunelius. Hoboken, NJ: Wiley, 2009.

The New Rules of Marketing & PR, by David Meerman Scott. Hoboken, NJ: Wiley, 2010.

Twitter for Dummies, by Laura Fitton and Michael Gruen. Hoboken, NJ: Wiley, 2009.

Twitter Power 2.0, by Joel Comm. Hoboken, NJ: Wiley, 2010.

TypePad for Dummies, by Melanie Nelson and Shannon Lowe. Hoboken, NJ: Wiley, 2010.

WordPress for Dummies, by Lisa Sabin-Wilson. Hoboken, NJ: Wiley, 2009.

Social Media Marketing Plan Worksheet

METHOD OF PARTICIPATION	TIME	ACTIVITY
Content creation		
Content sharing		
Connections		
Community building		

Glossary

blog: A website that contains entries (called posts) that are published in reverse chronological order and includes archives and social capabilities through comments published by visitors to the blog posts. Also called a *Web log* or *weblog*.

blog host: A company that provides space on its servers to store online content such as blogs and websites. Blog hosts may be free or paid. Also called *host* or *Web host*.

blog post editor: The section of an individual's blogging account dashboard where he or she can enter content to be published as blog posts. Also see *HTML editor* and *visual editor*.

blogging application: The program used by bloggers to create, maintain, and publish blogs. Examples are Blogger, WordPress, TypePad, and Movable Type.

brand: The tangible and intangible representation of a business or product, which includes a promise, message, and image.

browser: An application used to surf the Internet. Examples are Internet Explorer, Mozilla Firefox, Opera, Safari, and Google Chrome. Also called a *Web browser*.

comment: An opinion or thought written by a blog reader and published in response to a blog post. Comments typically appear at the end of a blog post. Not all blogs allow comments.

copyright: Legal ownership of a published work, including written text, art, music, and so on.

Creative Commons: A nonprofit organization that developed a series of less stringent copyright laws to enable publishers to more freely share their work.

cross-promotion: Marketing across various channels or businesses to achieve a common objective.

CSS: The acronym for Cascading Style Sheets, the language used to create blog layouts, designating the look and feel of a blog.

dashboard: The main page in a blogger's account within a blogging application where the blogger can manage all aspects of his or her blog.

domain name: The part of a URL that represents a specific website. For example, in *www .KeySplashCreative.com*, the domain name is *KeySplashCreative* plus the extension *.com*.

fair use: A gray area of copyright law that gives some leeway in how people can republish another person's work for the purposes of education, adding commentary, and news reporting.

feed: The syndicated content of a blog or website. The most common formats for syndicating online content are RSS and Atom.

feed reader: A tool used to aggregate and read feeds from websites and blogs to which a person subscribes.

forum: An online message board community where members post messages publicly and/or privately.

freelancer: An individual who independently offers services such as writing, Web design, Web development, programming, and more to clients.

FTP: The acronym for File Transfer Protocol, which is a process used to transfer files across the Internet from one computer or server to another.

host: See *blog host*.

HTML: The acronym for Hypertext Markup Language, which is a programming language that uses tags to create websites and blogs.

HTML editor: The option in a blog post editor that enables a blogger to enter content using HTML tags.

hyperlink: A virtual connection between two websites that, when clicked, takes the user to a different Web page. Also called a *link*.

integrated marketing: The process of creating multiple marketing tactics that work seamlessly together to reach a common objective.

keyword: A word or phrase used to contextually index a Web page so search engines can find it.

link: See *hyperlink*.

marketing strategy: A statement that defines a business's marketing direction and outlines how a business will achieve its marketing objectives.

marketing tactic: A specific effort or campaign executed in support of a marketing strategy to help a business reach its objectives.

microblogging: The process of publishing short snippets (usually 140 characters or fewer) to a personal profile using microblogging tools such as Twitter, Plurk, or Jaiku.

new media: Any form of nontraditional media born of Web 2.0, including blogs, microblogging, social networks, and so on.

niche: A specific and highly targeted segment of an audience or market. A niche blog is targeted at a very specific segment of a larger audience.

page rank: A ranking system used by search engines to determine a blog's or website's popularity and authority, which can affect a site's search engine rankings.

podcast: Serialized audio content that is recorded digitally for playback online.

pull marketing: A form of marketing where consumers demand and "pull" messages and interactions from businesses, rather than the businesses pushing messages at consumers.

push marketing: A form of marketing where businesses force and "push" messages and interactions at consumers, regardless of whether or not consumers want those messages and interactions with the business.

referrer: Any site or page that leads people to a blog (or another website) through a link on that site or page.

RSS: The acronym for Really Simple Syndication, which is the technology used to distribute online content in a format that is readable by feed readers.

search engine: A website used to search the Internet to find pages and sites related to the keywords. Popular search engines include Google, Yahoo! and Bing.

search engine optimization (SEO): The process of writing Web content, developing Web pages, and promoting online content to increase rankings for that content when people search for specific keywords.

search engine reputation management (SERM): The process of monitoring and analyzing search engine results for a specific keyword or keyword phrase to ensure the results delivered by the search engine are the results the business or individual wants people to see.

SEO: See *search engine optimization*.

SERM: See *search engine reputation management*.

sidebar: A column in a blog's layout that appears to the right, to the left, or flanking the widest column (where post content usually resides). Each blogger decides what he or she wants to include in a blog sidebar, but typically, sidebars include links to social media profiles, recent or popular posts, ads, and so on.

silo marketing: The process of creating marketing strategies and tactics that work independently with no consideration for other marketing activities implemented by that business.

social bookmarking: The process of saving and sharing links to Web pages for reference. Popular social bookmarking sites include Digg, StumbleUpon, and Delicious.

social media: Any form of publishing and communications media found on the social Web, including blogs, social networks, social bookmarking services, and microblogging.

social media marketing: Any form of marketing conducted using the tools of the social Web.

social networking: The process of communicating and interacting with other people online. Websites that provide social networking tools include Facebook and LinkedIn.

social Web: The second generation of the World Wide Web, which focuses on two-way conversation, interaction, communities, user-generated content, and relationships. Also called *Web 2.0*.

spam: A type of comment submitted on a blog for the express purpose of increasing links and driving traffic to a specific Web page. Spam e-mail is another common form of spam.

template: A predesigned blog layout created to make it easy for people with little to no technical knowledge to create a professional-looking blog. Also called a *theme*.

text link ad: A type of online ad that looks like a simple text link on a blog or website but is actually a link published in return for monetary compensation.

theme: See *template*.

trademark: An official registration provided by the U.S. Patent and Trademark Office that protects a name, logo, slogan, design, or other element so that only the trademark owner can use it within its industry.

traditional marketing: Any form of marketing that predates social media marketing—for example, advertising, direct mail, point-of-sale signage, sponsorships, and event marketing.

URL: The acronym for Uniform Resource Locator, which identifies the unique address of a specific page on the Internet. A complete URL may include an access protocol (for example, *http*), a domain name (for example, www.KeySplashCreative.com), and an extension designating a specific subpage within a site (for example, */specificpage.htm*).

visitor: A person who views at least one page on a website or blog.

visual editor: The option in a blog post editor that enables a blog-ger to enter content using a WYSIWYG (What You See Is What You Get) interface, which is similar to traditional word processing software.

vlog: A video blog post.

Web analytics: Statistics related to the performance of a website, blog, Web pages, and other online content.

Web host: See *blog host*.

Web log: See *blog*.

Web 2.0: See *social Web*.

WYSIWYG: The acronym for What You See Is What You Get.

References

Amtower, Mark. Interview by author. Telephone, February 23, 2010.

Delaney, Kelly. Interview by author. Telephone, February 25, 2010.

Isaacs, Liz. Interview by author. Telephone, March 1, 2010.

Jakubecy, Sharon. Interview by author. Telephone, February 22, 2010.

Quintana, Debbie. Interview by author. Telephone, February 26, 2010.

Schrementi, Daniel. Interview by author. Telephone, February 23, 2010.

Sinkin, Michael. Interview by author. Telephone, March 2, 2010.

Skriloff, Lisa. Interview by author. Telephone, February 22, 2010.

Thomas, Lorrie. Interview by author. Telephone, March 2, 2010.

Index

Note: Page numbers followed by *f* or *t* refer to figures or tables, respectively.

About the Author

Susan Gunelius is president and CEO of KeySplash Creative, Inc. (www.keysplashcreative.com), a full-service marketing communications company. She has nearly 20 years' experience working in the marketing field, with the first decade of her career spent directing marketing programs for some of the largest companies in the world, including divisions of AT&T and HSBC.

Susan is the author of over a half dozen business nonfiction books, including *Kick-Ass Copywriting in 10 Easy Steps*, *Building Brand Value the Playboy Way*, *Harry Potter: The Story of a Global Business Phenomenon*, *Blogging All-in-One for Dummies*, *Google Blogger for Dummies*, and *The Complete Idiot's Guide to WordPress*. She is a featured columnist for the online edition of *Entrepreneur* and a featured blogger for *Forbes*, and her marketing-related articles have appeared on the websites of MSNBC, Fox Business, the *Washington Post*, *BusinessWeek*, *SmartMoney*, *TheStreet*, and more. Susan often speaks at virtual and in-person events about marketing, branding, copywriting, and social media through her website at www.SusanGunelius.com.

Susan also owns one of the leading blogs for women working in the field of business, Women on Business (www.womenonbusiness.com), which has been named by *Forbes* as one of the top 100 blogs by women and one of the top 20 marketing and social media blogs. Women on Business was also a finalist in the 2009 Stevie Awards for Women in Business in the category of Best Blog.

Susan can be reached through her company website, www.keysplashcreative.com. You can connect with Susan on the social Web in the following places:

- **Blogs:** www.keysplashcreativeconversations.com *and* www.womenonbusiness.com

- **Facebook:** www.facebook.com/susangunelius *and* www.facebook.com/keysplashcreative
- **LinkedIn:** www.linkedin.com/in/susangunelius
- **Twitter:** www.twitter.com/susangunelius *and* www.twitter.com/womenonbusiness